The Parenting Exchange
A revolutionary parenting process that works!

Jennie Hernandez

Seven Stars

THE PARENTING EXCHANGE Copyright © 2013 by Seven Stars Inc

All rights reserved. No part of this book may be used or reproduced in any manner whatsoever without written permission from Seven Stars Inc, except as provided by the United States of America copyright law or in the case of brief quotations embodied in articles and/or reviews.

The scanning, uploading or distribution of this book via the Internet or any other means without the permission of the author is illegal and punishable by law.

Please purchase only authorized editions and do not participate in or encourage piracy of copyrighted materials. Your support of the author's rights is sincerely appreciated.

Printed in the United States of America

First Printing: 2013

ISBN: 978-0-9911399-4-1

Seven Stars

The

Parenting Exchange

Acknowledgments

I wish to thank first and foremost my wonderful children. It is because of you that this book is even here. You have been my anchor through all of my storms.

Also, many thanks to Lacar Musgrove who pulled this all together, Fernando Gutierrez for his support and great photography, Jeff Kahn for the creative cover work, Emily IsBell for her support and editing services, Cate Salinger for her encouragement and editing, Kurt Hanks who helped me with my first book and helped me to recognize that I could write.

A special thanks to my wonderful teacher and mentor Arthur Samuel Joseph. His integrity and wisdom inspire me daily.

Contents

Preface ix
Introduction 1
Section One: Searching for (and Finding) Answers 5
    Necessity--The Mother of Invention 7
    How the Exchanges Began 9
    Sensing a Sense of Entitlement 11
    The Big Meeting 13
    Making The Shift 14
Section Two: The Parenting Exchange 17
    The Parenting Exchange 19
    Principle I: All Relationships are Exchanges 21
    Principle II: Exchanges are Run by Expectations 27
    Principle III: Some Expectations Running Exchanges Are Hidden 41
    Principle IV: Bringing the Hidden Expectations Out on the Table Changes the Exchange 51
    Principle V: Focus on Getting the Exchange to Work, Not on Changing the Person 59
    Review: The Five Principles 73
Section Three: Making the Change 75

Parenting with Benefits ... 77
Parental Accountability ... 85
Section Four: Living the Exchange ... 91
    Putting it All Together ... 93
        You are in Charge ... 94
        You Can "Exchange" at Any Age ... 98
        Skills for the "Real World" ... 103
        A Dynamic Process ... 107
        Parenting on Purpose ... 114
        Benefits and Beyond (Home) ... 124
        A Different World (Than You Grew Up In) ... 130
        Applied Science (Fairs) ... 135
        A Different Process ... 142
Conclusion: It's Up to You ... 149

Preface

I did it! All seven of my children have graduated from high school. I've "raised" seven teenagers and now consider myself an *official* parenting expert. With this in mind, I would like to share with you an expanded version of my first book, *A Little Secret for Dealing with Teens*, which will provide more depth and insight from my perspective of today.

As the years have passed, I have learned the profound value of effective parenting—parenting that empowers, teaches self-sufficiency, and inspires children to be assured in who they are and to become adults who enjoy their lives and relationships, not only with others—but with themselves.

The Parenting Exchange shares the effective, integrative parenting process I created out of desperation as a single mother of seven living on welfare. At first, I turned to the parenting books of the day and found time-consuming and ineffective strategies. Eventually I discovered solutions by integrating business principles of exchange into my parenting. I made the connection that if these principles worked in the business world to create equity and value, they could have the same effect with my children. These principles will not only improve your relationship with your child but will help your child understand how to relate to others and the world after they "leave the nest."

My first book, as apparent by the title, was geared toward the parenting of teenagers. This new book is expanded to provide principles of parenting for children of any age. However, the older the child, the more interactive the exchange will be. I have also reworked the model of my "Principles of Exchange" to give more clarity and understanding while sharing a little more of my own journey as a parent to provide a clearer perspective of how this process worked for me and my children.

I hope that these principles and tools will be as effective for your family as they were for mine.

Introduction

Before becoming parents, we may envision parenting as taking care of cute little children and babies. We imagine how we can dress them and play with them and hope that they will be around us when we're confined to our rocking chairs during our twilight years. After decades of being a parent, I'm not going to say that this scenario isn't realistic, but there's a broader picture. It's kind of like when your kids ask to have a dog. "Oh, please mom!" they beg. "Can we have this puppy? She's so cute. She'll be so much fun and we *promise* that we'll take her for walks and feed her. You'll never have to do *anything*. We'll do it all," they assure. Well, if you have ever had this experience and got the dog, you will likely be able to testify that the outcome of this campaign was similar to what we experience from politicians after they become elected. Some of the promises are kept, but many are not.

With experiences such as this, you may have realized that your relationship with your child is not always equitable. Chances are that *you* have given the lion's share of time and energy in trying to make your relationship work. As a mother, I often felt that it was my "duty" to do as much for my children as possible, especially when circumstances were difficult. You

The Parenting Exchange

may feel obligated to provide for your child in the same way you perceive his or her friends' parents do. You want to ensure that your child has a better childhood than *you* had. Many of the driving forces behind our parenting methods are based on these kinds of beliefs that tend to be culturally or habitually driven. Perhaps you have not even questioned why you do what you do in your relationship with your child.

I discovered the *parenting exchange,* an interactive parenting process, when I was going through one of the most difficult times in my life: a crisis point. In the following pages, I will share with you this approach that I created. It not only saved my sanity as a mother but transformed my children's lives in amazing ways that I never believed possible.

This process incorporates a simple yet effective technique that can be used, as one parent described, "in spite of everything—whether you are single, divorced, or whatever your situation." It can help you deal with issues of child entitlement, "helicopter" parenting, and other matters of concern. The *parenting exchange* is a five-step interactive process that can be used in a variety of situations in your parenting relationships.

Necessity--The Mother of Invention

My children have been members of the National Honor Society, appeared in Who's Who Among High School Students, and won scholarships to the National Young Leaders Conference in Washington, D.C. My oldest son worked as a page in the Idaho State Legislature and is now a Princeton University graduate. They accomplished a lot, but what has been most important to me is recognizing the respect and love that my children developed for each other and for me. As adults, they are now responsible for their own lives. They are great people whom I love being around! Last year at Christmas, all five of my daughters were able to be home for the holiday. As a gift, I treated them to pedicures while I was at work. The next time I went into the nail shop, one of the workers mentioned that my girls had been there.

"You know that your girls do not seem like sisters," she commented.

"No?" I responded, somewhat puzzled.

"No," she said, "they seem more like best friends." It's true! Best friends is what they are with each other and with their brothers, too.

Initially, the reason I decided to write a parenting book was because so many people were asking me what I had done to make our family life so successful. Most were unaware of the circumstances we had been through. At parent-teacher conferences, my kids' teachers would say, "What did you do? Your child is one of the most responsible kids that I have in my class." Or she would say something like, "I wish all of the students in my class were like your child." I would explain, whether to the teachers or others who would ask, that I required an exchange with my kids. They were intrigued while wanting to know more. After I shared more of what I was doing, they would often suggest that I write a book. So I did.

This book describes the approach that I used and then later developed into a successful parenting process and parenting workshops. I subsequently developed a model-based approach that encompasses five effective and integrative principles of exchange. Many challenging situations that parents face can be "plugged-in" to the steps of this model to help uncover effective solutions. This method is based on a business-oriented, results-driven exchange approach, in which getting things to work well is the driving force.

As you use this approach, you will learn about and experience "equitable exchanges." You will begin to see your children assume more responsibility for their lives. They will learn to use their creative energy in positive ways that empower them in their relationships with their friends, siblings, adults and—in particular—with you. They will mature more gracefully and be ready for the world when it is time to leave home. Your life as a parent will become easier and *much* more pleasant.

Section One

Searching for (and Finding)

Answers

Necessity--The Mother of Invention

"Necessity is the mother of invention." So the saying goes. Several years ago, I had a need that was so great that I felt desperate to find a solution. My family life was out of control. My children were highly "at risk" (according to the statistics) for dropping out of school, bad grades, and *much* more. As I share my story with you, I hope it will inspire you to see the possibilities within your own family, no matter what circumstances you find yourself in. Let me take you there...

I had been raised in a large religious family where I believed, to my core, that I would always be married and would stay home to raise my children. I loved being a mom! I thought that my husband would always provide for our family and I would be secure as a stay-at-home mom. Guided by this belief, I left college at nineteen to marry and start my family.

Fast forward several years later. My husband and I filed for bankruptcy and, two years later, were divorced. I wasn't prepared for what lay ahead of me. My youngest of seven children was one year old and my oldest was sixteen. Up to this point, I had never had a full-time job and still had no college degree, having supported my husband while he got his. After the divorce, I was granted full custody of my seven children.

My ex-husband paid me one month of child support and told me that I would receive no more from him. With seemingly no other options, I walked to the welfare office (I had no car at the time) to enroll and begin my new life as a single mother.

Around this same time, my landlady told me that we needed to leave the house. (In my opinion, it was because there would now be no man around to fix things up for free.) Within a year, I moved out of state with my seven children. I had no marketable job skills, so I enrolled in school as a full-time student. This was tough for me for many reasons, including having to put my youngest children in daycare—something I had never done before. All the change and disruption was confusing not only for me but especially for my children. They were unhappy and became angry and resentful. I could see in their eyes and hear in their words how they felt: *It's all your fault, Mom, that we're in this mess!*

My children did not deal well with the chaos that was everywhere in their lives. Within the first few weeks after I started back to school, things went wrong. I was overwhelmed by my responsibilities: tackling schoolwork, learning how to use a computer for the first time, commuting an hour each way to and from school, keeping up with my house, and trying all the while to be a "good" mom. I was doing almost all of the household and parenting tasks. Whenever anything in the house broke, I fixed it. Whenever the kids had to go somewhere, I took them. The responsibility for raising seven children was mine alone, and it wasn't working.

Necessity—The Mother of Invention

I was running ragged and felt like I was losing all control of my home and the relationships with my children. It seemed the harder I tried, the worse it became. The kids were becoming more defiant and expecting me to "fix" *everything*. They were angry. Policemen were showing up at my door. It became apparent to me that I couldn't keep a handle on everything by doing things the way I had done in the past. The path my kids were headed down needed to be altered, fast.

All of this was weighing heavily on my mind. I knew deep inside that things had to change. I was compelled to take a step back and gain some perspective—so that's what I did. I didn't want my children's lives to suffer because of some of my past decisions. I wanted to help them have lives that were better than mine and hoped to provide them with the tools to empower themselves. I needed to find a way to accomplish this despite my uncertain circumstances. I wasn't going to give up until I discovered a solution.

Over the next several weeks, finding a way to help my children was my constant endeavor. First, I turned to the "experts." The "experts," as I soon learned, often gave complicated, long-winded instructions on how to raise children. Surprisingly, many had no firsthand experience. For example, one self-proclaimed expert I saw on a talk show had a lot of academic credentials but had never been married or had any kids. He had *a few* good ideas, but I couldn't even begin to relate to him (nor him to me, I'm sure). Despite my doubts about the "experts," I frequented the library (Internet information was much more limited at the time) checking out books that promised answers but never seemed to get to the point. I remember one book in particular (one of the better ones, actually) that went through a twelve-step, three-day process on cooperative problem-solving, with page after page of technical explanations. All I was thinking as I read through them was that during those three days even more problems would develop and I wouldn't know how to keep track of the problems I had started out with! Not very helpful. I didn't have the time or patience to read through it all or to try to apply it. There had to be a better way, I thought—one that a busy, pressured parent like myself could use without being overwhelmed.

How the Exchanges Began

When I first became a single parent, one of my biggest dilemmas was trying to be all things to all of my kids. Despite the impossibility of doing this, my children seemed to expect it without question. I desperately needed to overcome this expectation—but how?

I didn't have the time or resources to give in to the many demands of my children, nor did I want to blindly leave them to their own devices. I was parenting alone and away from my children most of the time. At times, all I wanted was to get through the day without a disaster.

As I shared before, at this time I was a full-time college student enrolled in a vocational program in business management. Despite all the demands I was facing, I quite

Necessity—The Mother of Invention

enjoyed my business classes. One of those classes was a basic economics class. My professor introduced to me concepts such as scarcity, value, exchange, equity, and results. I absorbed this new information like a sponge. A successful business, I learned, is results driven. In business, the bottom line is achieving results while getting things accomplished efficiently *and* effectively.

Then a light came on in my mind: why can't I apply these same principles to my parenting? If anyone understood scarcity, I did: scarcity of money, scarcity of time, scarcity of information. I also needed results! Recognizing that business theories are generally biased towards performance and results—not necessarily concerned with the "why" of things—I correlated the principles of business management with the problems of parenting. A business manager typically has more experience, knowledge, and expertise than does a lower-level employee. Parents are in a similar position with their children. A manager has more access to company resources and is in a position of power, like a parent is. Like an effective manager, a successful parent needs to have the benefit of the whole always in mind. As I contemplated these concepts, the business principles I was learning at school seemed more applicable than all those child development theories I had researched.

How could I use the business principles that I was learning in school to solve my parenting problems? How could I achieve the effective results I was looking for? Over the next few months, I used the principles of business to formulate a new way to work with my children. My primary goal was to get my family up and running effectively while taking a substantial load off of me. At the time I had no idea how successful or effective this process would be.

Sensing a Sense of Entitlement

As I tried to come up with a plan to help my children, I left myself open to hear my "inner voice." Also, I focused on specific issues that I needed to deal with. I watched and listened to what my kids were doing and saying. The following story demonstrates one of these times and how I had one of my "aha" moments.

Paul, my then seventeen-year-old son, began to complain about needing nicer clothes and more access to the family car. He was upset with me over what he saw as my neglect. He sent me subtle and not-so-subtle messages—a word here and a comment there. And then there was that *look*. I was falling into the trap of guilt, which was exacerbated by my being either gone from the house or busy most of the time.

At first I felt that I should comply with my son's demands, but then it dawned on me, *how is this fair to me?* So, I invited Paul to sit down with me to discuss the matter of my neglect. I suggested that we make a list of the expectations we had of each other. My list went something like this: Paul wanted me to furnish him with a room of his own and restrict access by other family members. He wanted unrestricted use of the family car—fully fueled, repaired, and always clean. He wanted me to pay the car insurance, which was dramatically more expensive because he was driving my car. He also wanted free access to

Necessity--The Mother of Invention

my computer and the Internet connection. He expected me to buy his clothes, but of course only the clothes he approved of. (His shoes needed to be a certain brand and style, including special shoes for each of the sports he played.) I was expected to do all of his laundry, including those times he urgently needed that special T-shirt washed, and I was expected to shop for groceries, cook, and serve him all of his meals.

Another victim of the narcissistic mentality

Pointing to the list (which he didn't disagree with), I asked him, "What do I get in exchange for all this?" I saw shock covering his face. He was speechless. I continued. "So I guess what you're saying to me is that I'm supposed to give all this to you, in exchange for which you bless me with your presence in our home?"

"Well, y..y..yeah!! He stammered, wide-eyed and innocent.

"Would *you* like to be on the other end of an exchange like this one?" I asked.

First he looked at me, then he stared into space. He could see I wasn't going to go on until he responded. Finally he admitted, "Well, no, I wouldn't."

What dawned on me was that my children had a sense of entitlement, despite the extremely limited resources of our family. It also became clear that I had unknowingly contributed to these expectations throughout their lives.

Over that past few years, I have talked to a lot of parents, experts, and others about this issue of "entitlement." It seems to be prevalent in our culture for some reason. I believe the biggest reason is that parents behave and exchange with their children in a way that demonstrates to them that they *are* entitled—just because they are kids.

Recognizing that this sense of entitlement was at the root of our family's problems, I began to envision a method that would incorporate business principles into my parenting. In the business world, when you don't have the money to get what you need, you get creative. That is what I did. I knew that my kids and I could and should help each other. I recognized the value of *exchange*. My thinking was that since every member of the family had skills, energy, and needs, we could initiate exchanges to enable each of us to get what we needed. Eventually, this led to my principle-based parenting exchange model, which proved to be more effective than I could have ever imagined.

The Big Meeting

During the next few weeks, I collected my thoughts and made notes of how I would introduce this new way of life to my children. Andy, my youngest, was only 2, while Paul, my oldest, was 17 and my five daughters, Juliana, Linda, Aleena, Emily, and Christina were in between. I wasn't sure how effective my new plan would be since my children's ages and needs were so diverse. Even so, I gathered the kids (which felt a bit like herding cats) for the family meeting.

Once we were somewhat settled, I made the big announcement:

Necessity--The Mother of Invention

"Kids, we need to talk." I began. "From now on, we will be doing things differently. I can't keep doing everything for our family by myself. From now on, whenever you need me to do something for you, you will need to do something for me, in exchange, first. The reason I'll need you to do this is so I will have more time and energy to help you get what you need from me."

I was met with mixed reactions. Of course my preschoolers really didn't have a clue of what I was explaining. The teenagers didn't *want* to have a clue of what was going on and the "in-between" ages just kind of sat there. I continued to explain what I had envisioned. "Doing this will be a learning process for all of us. What I will expect of the little ones will, of course, be different than what you older kids will need to do. So, next time you need me to do something for you, you can ask me what would be something you could do for me in exchange, and I'll give you some ideas."

This was the beginning of totally new relationships within our family.

Making The Shift

For the first twenty years of your child's life, you will have about seventy-three hundred days to spend with him or her—plenty of time in which to experiment and try something new when things aren't working. I've heard that the definition of insanity is to keep doing the same thing over and over while expecting different results. Yet that's what I see many parents doing with their kids—the same thing over and over, expecting the relationship to improve.

I know what it is like to feel as if I'm failing with my kids, even after my best efforts. I know what it is like to want a better relationship with my children and a better family life and not know how to get it. *And* I really know how hard it is to try something new. So, if what you're doing in your relationship with your child isn't working as well as you'd like, maybe it's time for a change. My approach to dealing with my children was to try something completely different. It worked for me and I believe it can work for you, too.

> **If what you're doing isn't working, try something different.**

A Simple Shift in Focus

As my family began to live these principles, our lives changed like magic. At the time, I didn't have a clue that the results would be so amazing. After many years of using this process, I now have the perspective to see how and why this worked. By shifting the focus to the ***exchange,*** rather than on the individual, your relationships will transform. The principles that follow will guide you on how to implement this process of exchange. This simple concept of exchange can affect a major shift in your relationships as well as help your child gain valuable life skills along the way.

Section Two

The Parenting Exchange

The Parenting Exchange

Here are the five principles of exchange. Each one builds on the principle before it:

1. All relationships are exchanges.

2. Exchanges are run by expectations.

3. Some expectations running exchanges are hidden.

4. Bringing the hidden expectations "out-on-the-table" changes the exchange.

5. Focus on getting the exchange to work, not on changing the other person.

The following chapters will illustrate each principle through stories and examples. One of the great features of this principle-based model is that it is context-based. When issues arise with your child, you can plug in the context of your dilemma and run it through this process.

For example, during one of my parenting seminars, a parent asked what he could do about his daughter's constant lying. I couldn't really help him with this general problem, so I asked him for a specific situation where his daughter had lied to him. We then went through the process of inserting this specific incident into the steps of these principles and identified an effective solution.

So let's start....

Principle I

All Relationships are Exchanges

All Relationships Are Exchanges.

The relationship you have with your child is an exchange.

Parent  Child

You give to your child and may or may not expect something in return.

Your child expects from you and may or may not give something back in return.

Exchanges

Picture yourself shopping at your favorite grocery store. While there, you discover that there are no prices posted anywhere. After you fill your cart with groceries and take it to the checkout counter, the clerk scans your items and charges your debit card without telling you what you spent. How long would you continue shopping at that store? The reason we shop at a particular store and return to shop there again is because we have agreed on an exchange: established prices for the products we purchase. We benefit from the exchange, and so does the merchant. We are able to shop with confidence because we know in advance what the exchange is.

> **All of your relationships are *already* exchanges**

Most parents, in their relationships with their children, are like shoppers at the imaginary "no prices" grocery store. They engage in exchanges with their children without ever looking at the cost involved.

I'm not asking you to turn your relationships into exchanges; I'm asking you to recognize that all of your relationships are *already* exchanges. We engage in exchanges with grocers, bankers, hairdressers, teachers, spouses, kids, pets, and others. We exchange commodities such as money, goods, services, time, energy, and companionship. We also exchange less quantifiable things such as friendship, love, and fulfillment. Regardless of the content of the exchange, all of our relationships involve some kind of exchange. Let's look at some common exchanges.

Friendship Exchanges

Cathy has been my friend for years. Our exchange is easy to see. We have shared similar experiences in our lives. We understand each other and can talk for hours together. I have used her as a sounding board to help me work out problems or concerns I have, and she does the same with me. Cathy has been the only friend I have had at times and has helped me through some rough experiences. I have done the same for her. We may not have contact for months at a time, but with a phone call we immediately start again where we left off. Our friendship works because we each benefit from the exchange. I've helped her; she's helped me. I listen to her; she listens to me. Our equitable interaction has made our friendship endure.

Neighbor Exchanges

Years ago, when my daughter Christina was seven, I noticed an enjoyable exchange that she had with her friend Michelle from down the street. The two little girls had become very good friends. Michelle was an only child—quite a contrast from our large family. When they visited each other's houses, each girl got something she didn't have at home. At our house, Michelle loved the interaction of lots of kids and the chaos that always seemed to be a part of our home. Christina, on the other hand, loved to go to Michelle's house to play alone with just her friend, and not all of her brothers and sisters. While their friendship may have had its ups and downs, in the long run Michelle and Christina each benefited from the exchange.

Community Exchanges

Here's a unique exchange which I learned about from my grandmother, who lived in a small rural town most of her life. A local barber had been cutting hair for many years. His fees were reasonable for everyone, but there was one gentleman customer whom he never charged. After many years of wondering why this man didn't pay for his haircuts, my grandmother finally asked the barber why. He knew her well, so, after swearing her to secrecy, he told her. There was an unspoken exchange between the barber and this customer, who knew *all* the gossip in the county. As the barber *slowly* cut his hair, the gentleman shared all the latest gossip. For the next month, the barber in turn would share this gossip with his other customers. And he had some very loyal customers—because they also wanted to know what was going on locally. Everybody benefited, except those who were being gossiped about!

The Parenting Exchange

Nature Exchanges

We can also find beneficial exchanges in nature. The Egyptian plover, better known as the "crocodile bird," has an interesting exchange with the crocodile. The crocodile actually lets this bird get into its mouth and pick out bits of food and leaches from its teeth, like a feathered toothbrush. The crocodile benefits by having clean teeth; the bird benefits by getting food.

Here are some examples of typical, everyday exchanges: *If you sew my dress, I'll babysit. If you wash, I'll put away. If you scratch my back, I'll scratch yours* . . . .. You get the idea.

Principle II

Exchanges are Run by Expectations

Exchanges Are Run By Expectations.

Parent's Expectation:
If I give you a room, the least you can do is keep it clean.

Child's Expectation:
It's my room and I can do anything I want with it.

Expectations

In my first parenting book, I used the word *rule* rather than *expectation* in this context. When I taught this concept, I realized that how I was using this word was different from how many people understood it. After a lot of thinking, I settled on the word *expectation* instead. My reasons will become clearer as you move into the next steps.

In every exchange, each person has his or her own expectations. Most of the time, we are unaware of these expectations—it's just how we operate. This is true for every relationship we have. While it is easy to see this in impersonal exchanges such as financial transactions, buying a car, or getting a loan, it is harder to see the expectations that govern the emotional exchanges we have with family and friends. But no matter the relationship, the expectations of the exchange are always there, directing the interaction. They may be sensible or crazy, but either way they run all of our relationships—especially those we have with our children.

Here are some examples of expectations that shape our everyday interactions:

- If I'm polite, people will like me.
- If you keep buying me things, I will continue to be your friend.

The Parenting Exchange

- When I lose weight, I will be happier.
- I only deserve to be in a relationship with someone who treats me poorly.
- *The Boss*: "If I praise your work, you will work harder."
- *The Employee*: "I can clock in a few minutes late each day and still get my full amount of pay."

Here are a few examples of expectations in parenting relationships:

Parent: "I'll give you what you want, but in return you will love and respect me."
Child: It's a parent's job to do everything for me.
Mother: "Since I'm your mom, I'll always know what's best for you."
Child: Everything my parents have will eventually be mine.
Parent: "Since I was deprived as a child, I will ensure that this never happens to my children."
Child: I can use my parents as scapegoats for my failures and problems in life.
Parent: I owe my kids the experience of becoming self-sufficient adults who can think and act for themselves.

These are just a few examples of expectations that you may have heard or experienced. You should now see that your everyday actions (that are often unconscious) and interactions start with these types of expectations. Then, most of the time, we behave in ways that reinforce these expectations.

What We Owe Our Children

I believe that a parent owes a child the basic necessities of food, shelter, clothing, nurturing, and love. Beyond the basics, everything else should be worked out through an exchange. My kids need clothes, and they should be given those clothes regardless of what they do or don't do for me. But designer clothes are a different story, and an equitable exchange needs to be worked out to get these. My kids must eat, but again, eating *out* is another thing—an exchange must be arranged. These are some of my expectations in regard to my children.

Some parents I've seen give and give and give to their children until they are empty, only to turn around and give some more. Their children don't ever seem to think about what they could or should give in return. I know of one mother who repeatedly hands money to her son, only to have him swear at her because it is not enough. Respect should be part of the exchange—appreciation, too. This mother gets neither. Her expectation may be the opposite of mine, which is probably something like this: *My son should have all he needs and wants, and I am a failure if I can't provide him with that.*

Along these same lines, I remember one father's comments to his son who had repeatedly insulted him in front of others at a family reunion. The father, looking puzzled at his son's behavior, asked, "If you treated your friends like you treat me,

The Parenting Exchange

how long would your friends be your friends?" It was evident that this son's expectation about friendship didn't apply to the relationship he had with his father.

Entitlement

The unspoken expectations that underlie many parent-child exchanges are often one-sided. If you wrote down these expectations and showed them to some parents, they probably wouldn't believe anyone in their right mind would have such one-sided interactions. In fact, they'd probably think that someone who followed such twisted thinking was foolish. Here are some illustrations of what I'm talking about.

> **The unspoken expectations that underlie many parent-child exchanges are often one-sided.**

Between one father and his teenage son, the expectations go something like this:

Teen: *Whatever trouble I get into, my dad will get me out of it.*

Complementing the teen's expectation is the father's expectation: *I will fix any of my son's mistakes; he is just a kid and needs the best start possible in his life.*

These two expectations driving the relationship between father and son have led to some interesting, heated exchanges with the police. I don't think the police have the same

Expectations

expectations as either father or son. The police are probably thinking something like this: *Lock this kid up and lose the key. Keep the father quiet and hide his wallet; then things will be much safer and quieter for the rest of us.*

An underlying expectation that many kids have is: *I get to decide what is best in my relationship with my parent.* Again, these expectations are often unconscious. I have seen children become angry because, for some reason, they have learned that they have the right to be in charge and expect mom or dad to conform to their agenda. Many times, the parents' actions have instilled this idea in their child. I'm not saying that the needs of children should not be met or that they shouldn't get the things that they want, just that an equitable exchange should be set by both parties, while the parent is still in charge.

A friend of mine had a teenage daughter who, for many years, had a pretty good life. Their family life was comfortable, financially sound, and so on. Things were going well until the father became unemployed. Suddenly things weren't so rosy. The daughter had never experienced not getting the things she wanted. Her parents were now under considerable stress and tempers were short. After several weeks of this, the daughter was not coping very well. Until this time, her expectation was something like: *Everything should always be good; if it's not then I can do whatever I want to, to compensate, regardless of how it affects those around me.* One day a friend at school told her she had some pot and wanted her to smoke it with her. She complied, thinking this might be a good way to deal with her emotions, feeling justified in doing this because of the problems at home. She gave no thought as to what consequences her actions may have for others, particularly her parents. Her actions only ended up causing considerably more stress at home, as the girls were caught smoking the pot.

When setting exchanges, something to remember is that you have many valuable resources to give your child. Your time, money, attention, and friendship are just a few. When I exchange with my children, one priceless commodity that I value from them is respect. I also enjoy the friendship they have willingly given me. In return, I respect them and treat them in ways I would treat my friends. I don't intentionally use or impose my will on my friends, so I make it a point to respect my children in this same way. Friendship without respect isn't real friendship.

Acquiring Expectations

By now you have probably figured out that I created this parenting process out of necessity as a mom. I'm sure that a psychologist could provide much more scientific and researched answers to the question of where and how we acquire our expectations that run our exchanges. From the perspective of my experiences, I believe that you simply acquire the expectations that run your exchanges from your past exchanges.

All exchanges teach expectations. As we interact or exchange in life, we learn the rules that underlie our thinking. We interact with family, school, the media, and more. From

Expectations

infancy, our exchanges with our children are teaching them what to expect from us. And as our children get older, they will absorb more and more from other places, much of it subliminally. Watching television may teach your child that all of life's problems can be comfortably resolved in thirty or sixty minutes. He may pick up from playing computer games that he is indestructible. So, on and on we go, gathering our expectations as we move through life, then expressing them in all our relationships. We are always picking up our expectations through our exchanges.

> **All exchanges teach expectations.**

For example, let's look at one husband's "standing-in-line" expectation. Years ago, I attended an educational conference where the majority of attendees were women. Before one of the classes began, I was standing in line when a man in front of me smiled and began chatting. We talked for a minute or two, and then he asked me, "What class is this?" Smiling, trying to hold back a laugh, I said to him, "Well, this is the women's restroom." First shock then total embarrassment spread across his face. Turning away he mumbled, "Oh, I just follow my wife wherever she goes." He then quickly wandered off to find another line. Just blindly following his wife is what this man learned from interacting with her—possibly because he expects her to always know best and lead him around.

I know that some parents of young children are convinced that all they do for their child will be beneficial. They are constantly taking their child to ball games, athletic practices, music lessons, parties, and movies. This is great, but as parents do this, they need to be aware that they are also teaching their child expectations. Here are some potential impressions: *Mom or dad should let me do all the things I want and provide the means to do these things. What I need and want to do is most important.* Now that this child has learned these expectations, what happens when a thirteen-year-old daughter wants to go with a seventeen-year-old classmate in his new car? Even though the parent sees that this is probably not going to be very beneficial for the daughter, the daughter expects her parents to let her do everything that she wants. When these "first-time" scenarios confront parents, they are often surprised at the response from their child when they put on the brakes—also for the first time—when the child is operating on the expectation she has been taught up to this point.

Identifying Expectations

Now that you are aware that your child's behaviors are based on expectations learned from past exchanges, how do you begin to identify what those expectations are?

The best way to understand this is to watch for patterns of behavior. For example, I heard my daughter's little friend say to her: "If you liked me, you wouldn't go to Melissa's house; you would only come to mine." She says variations of this to all her playmates. This little girl's expectation is exclusivity in her friendships. Or take the example of kids after they get home from trick-or-treating. When they start to eat all of their candy,

Expectations

they expect: *If a little bit of something is good, then a lot of it is even better.* Later in life this very same expectation resurfaces: *If I like Chinese food, then the all-you-can-eat buffet will be even better.* How many of us now wish we could follow Mary Poppins' rule: "Enough is as good as a feast"?

Here is an illustration of how a simple expectation can be totally opposite between a parent and a child.

> Your child may think: *My bedroom is just that, mine. I can do whatever I want with it. I don't have to clean it, and I can have any of my friends over with the door closed because it's my room.*

> You may think: *This is my house. I pay the bills. My child's room is in my home so I can decide what happens in that room.*

Each person feels justified in his expectation. You could easily recognize how conflict may develop from these opposing expectations.

If you begin to watch your child's behaviors closely, you will see the patterns of his expectations. I don't see most expectations as particularly bad or good, but I do see them as either working or not working.

Try a Test!

Do you know what expectations govern your exchanges with your child? What expectations do you have of your child? What expectations does he or she have of you?

Take some time to answer the following questions. What do *you* think your expectations are for dealing with your child? What do you think your *child's* expectations are when interacting with you? Using this list will help you as we continue through the steps.

What are your expectations within your relationship with your child?

1. _____

_____

2. _____

_____

3. _____

_____

The Parenting Exchange

What do you think are your child's expectations within his or her relationship with you?

1. _____

   _____

2. _____

   _____

3. _____

   _____

Once you begin to identify the expectations governing the exchanges with your child, you should keep using them only if you are getting good results. If you're not getting the results you want, start identifying and changing the expectations of the exchange. Principle Three will show you how.

Principle III

Some Expectations Running Exchanges Are Hidden

Some Expectations Running Exchanges Are Hidden.

Some expectations are out in the open and on the table: *"Since I pay the bills, you should keep your room clean."*

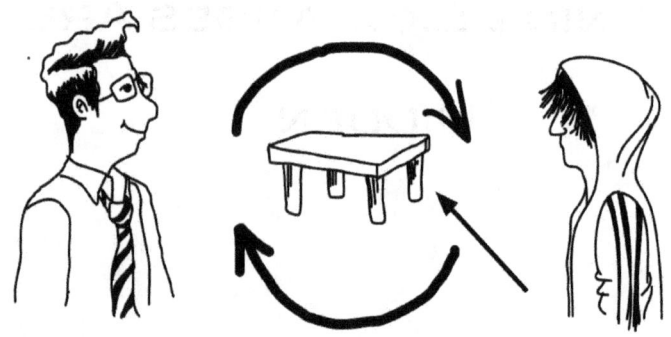

Some expectations are hidden and under the table: The child thinks, *You owe me because you're the parent and that's what parents are for.*

Hidden Expectations and Agendas

Some of the most important expectations governing our exchanges (relationships) are hidden, and we are unaware of them. They are unstated assumptions about what we expect of ourselves and others. When our children operate according to hidden expectations, they have little awareness of those expectations that may be buried deep in their subconscious. Or they may be vaguely aware of a hidden expectation without recognizing it for what it is. (However, there may be times when they have a hidden agenda and purposely keep that hidden from you.)

Hidden expectations frequently have more power over relationships than "out-in-the-open" ones.

Hidden expectations frequently have more power over relationships than do "out-in-the-open" ones. They may operate independently of any conscious effort and can control the parent-child relationship even more than an "out-in-the-open" agreement. These can invisibly direct both the parent and child and cause problems and conflicts to persist.

Let me share with you a story from when I was in high school. When I was fifteen, I kept finding myself in an

The Parenting Exchange

unresolvable situation with my mother. If it was Saturday, my work was never done. My mother gave me jobs such as vacuuming or folding clothes. I did my chores with the expectation that I could do my own thing—such as watching television or whatever I wanted to do—when I finished. But when I *had* finished and was sitting on the couch watching TV, she would come into the room and give me another job to do.

Finally, one Saturday morning, I came up with an idea that I thought would prevent this from happening again. I asked my mom to write down a list of *all* of the chores she needed me to complete that day. After she wrote down the list, I confirmed with her to ensure that she had written down *all* of my jobs for the day. She did so and agreed that these were all of my jobs. Just to make sure, I confirmed that when I finished this list, I would be free to go and do whatever I wanted such as watch TV or even just do nothing. Again, she said yes. Well, you may be able to guess how this turned out. When I finished my jobs for the day, I went to watch TV. Within a few minutes, yep, she had another job for me. I remained frustrated, never knowing how to solve this.

Today, I understand the hidden expectation that governed our exchange. My mother's hidden expectation—hidden, I believe, even from herself—was that *everyone should always be busy and not waste time.* In her mind, watching TV or even resting was a waste of time. My expectation conflicted with her expectation; I figured that after I got my work done, I should be free to stare at the ceiling if I wanted to. Having had this experience with my mother, I made it a point to give my

Bringing the Hidden Expectations Out on the Table Changes the Exchange

children time and permission to express how they felt in their exchanges with me. I also let them bring any of *my* hidden expectations out in the open. This is a vital step in creating *equitable* exchanges.

What's Boiling Underneath

Let me relate to you some real-life instances of exchanges involving some people I've know. (These aren't their real names.) These scenarios will illustrate how hidden expectations affect relationships.

Beating Up Dad

Rob, who was nineteen, had been living on his own for a year. During his absence, his father, Steve, had divorced and remarried. Steve and his new wife, Tara, invited Rob to live with them while he attended school at a nearby community college. Rob accepted the invitation. Steve and Tara provided him with tuition money as well as room and board. They also gave him a pickup truck to drive, along with gasoline, insurance, and repair money. In addition, Steve hired Rob to work for him on weekends in his construction business. This was a great deal for Rob. But there was a hidden catch. Steve was very active in their local church. He and Tara had an unspoken expectation of Rob to behave as a model child and to

The Parenting Exchange

demonstrate to the community their success as a Christian family. This was their hidden expectation.

Rob, on the other hand, had no idea that this expectation was part of the exchange, since Steve and Tara had never openly expressed it. Perhaps he was supposed to have gotten it through the subtle messages they sent. Steve and Tara, on the other hand, probably had no conscious awareness of their expectations and had just assumed that Rob would conform.

Consequently, Steve and Tara became increasingly frustrated and upset when Rob stayed out late at night with his friends, refused to attend church with them, and more. Rob became the target of most of their conversations as they analyzed everything he was and wasn't doing. One day Tara confronted Rob, insisting that he attend church, participate in family activities, and arrive home by 10:30 on weeknights. Rob, used to being on his own, resisted. Steve overheard the argument and joined in, taking Tara's side. The more they insisted, the angrier Rob became. As the argument escalated, Rob couldn't hold it in any more. He became so furious that he beat up his father. Steve ended up in the hospital with bruises and broken ribs. It took weeks for him to recuperate. Steve and Tara demanded that their wayward son leave the house.

Such violence was out of character for Rob. Why was he so angry? I believe it was because the terms of the exchange were so deeply hidden that he had no way even to discuss them. Prior to this, when Rob tried to defend his position, it would always end in an argument with Rob being wrong. So, things kept boiling up inside of Rob. With no way to acknowledge or

Bringing the Hidden Expectations Out on the Table Changes the Exchange

vent what was happening to him, Rob exploded. If Steve and Tara had told him up front what they expected of him in exchange for their generosity, he could have decided for himself, in advance, whether he wanted to accept the conditions attached to their gifts. As it was, their generosity was a trap.

> **Hidden expectations, rules, and agendas only complicate and disrupt healthy relationships.**

This story may seem extreme, but if there are hidden agendas, children feel trapped. They constantly seem to be in trouble, and they aren't even sure what they have done. This is what makes this step of the process so valuable to a working relationship with your child. It gives you a tool to see where some of the conflict and "rebellion" may start.

Hidden expectations, rules, and agendas only complicate and disrupt healthy relationships.

The Family Counselor's Family

Cynthia, a counselor and family therapist who occasionally gives presentations at seminars on parenting, is the mother of two teenage daughters. She holds an unspoken expectation that parents should continually give to their children with no expectation of return. Her new husband, Ray, struggling in his equally new role as a stepfather, operates under a similar idea: *I want my stepdaughters to like me, so I will give them whatever they want,*

The Parenting Exchange

whenever they want it. The girls had been living like princesses: trips to Mexico and Disneyworld, nice clothes, lots of spending money.

Late one evening, the girls arrived at their house with two rough-looking boyfriends and asked for some money and the keys to the car. Their intention was to buy booze and get drunk with their friends. Ray handed over the keys to his new car, gave them a handful of money out of his wallet and sent them on their way with a warning: "Be home before daylight." (He wasn't joking.) The girls had an accident with the car that night; fortunately, no one was seriously injured, but the car was totaled.

Cynthia continues to present herself professionally as an expert on parenting even though her own children's lives have been out of control. Ray's strategy to get the girls to like him failed. Eventually one stepdaughter moved out to live on her own; the other moved in with her natural father. In this exchange, the parents foolishly assumed responsibility for the consequences of their daughters' conduct, and the daughters took advantage of their parents' generous expectations. In the end, neither the parents nor the daughters got what they really needed or wanted.

"In a Minute!"

There are times when people intentionally hide their expectations. This can happen when someone expresses what I call a "statement of intent." If a statement of intent is not

Bringing the Hidden Expectations Out on the Table Changes the Exchange

congruent with the actual intention, this statement can confuse or mislead the other person in the relationship. Let me explain.

How many times will a parent ask a child to do a quick job such as taking out the trash, only to have him reply "I will in a minute"? I'm sure many parents can relate to this experience. The child's statement of intent is that he will respond to the request sometime in the future. The parent may expect that he will do the job when it's more convenient for him. But perhaps the real intention of the child is not to do the job, and he expects that if he puts it off enough times, he can get out of doing it. In this type of scenario, the parents may read the intention of the child as being willing and therefore expect the child to eventually do the job, but the child's hidden agenda may be just the opposite.

I was recently talking to a friend about this process. She told me about a friend of hers, Matt, who was having a hard time with his son who had just completed his freshman year at college. Apparently this young man's grades were not very good, and he had done a lot of drinking and partying. She said that Matt had given his son everything he "needed," such as a new car, an apartment, money, and so on. In questioning my friend about why Matt gave all of this to his son, she said that he didn't know what else to do. He had felt very guilty about not spending enough time with his son and wanted to make it up to him. Again, a statement of intent hiding the real agenda. If Matt was sincere in his motivation, why didn't he just spend more time with his son? If Matt was not willing or able to spend more time with his son, why didn't he simply tell his son that

The Parenting Exchange

and let him know that he couldn't spend time and that the only thing he had to offer was money? Matt expected money to be a reasonable substitute for his time.

Don't be blinded by statements of intent. You will be better able to read people's intentions if you watch their *actions*, rather than relying on what they *say*. By observing the actions of your children, you will be able to recognize their true expectations within your relationship. In the next step, we will look at how to bring these hidden expectations "out on the table."

Principle IV

Bringing the Hidden Expectations Out on the Table Changes the Exchange

Bring the Hidden Expectations "Out on the Table"

Put all the hidden expectations out on the table and talk about them.

Hidden expectations can sabatoge your intention of having an efffective relationship with your child.

Bringing Out Hidden Expectations

As long as expectations remain hidden, they will control the relationship—usually in ways that produce conflict. If you want an immediate change, the best way to do it is to bring hidden expectations out in the open—all of them. Examine them, laugh at them (if appropriate) and change them (if necessary). The benefits that follow will be greater than you might expect.

The following example from the family of a close friend will illustrate what I'm talking about:

If you want an immediate change, the best way to do it is to bring hidden expectations out in the open.

When David was about thirteen, he tended to object whenever things didn't go his way. Consistently, his objection contained the words, "That's not fair!" When asked to take out the garbage, he responded, "That's not fair; I have to do more work than my brothers and sisters."

It was the same when treats were divided among the children: "That's not fair; they got more ice cream than I did." He had a hidden expectation that work and treats would be divided evenly, and that any inequity would be in his favor. If he got more stuff or did less work than someone else, that was just fine, but if he got less stuff or did more work

The Parenting Exchange

than someone else, it wasn't fair. He was blind to the fact that in the long run, things like goodies and chores tended to even out. Eventually his father sat down with him and helped him to identify this expectation so he could examine it. Once it was brought out in the open, he dropped it. He never again insisted, "That's not fair."

By putting expectations on the table where everyone can see them, you can address what is really going on in your home. Many parents get frustrated when trying to work out situations with their kids, especially as kids get older. (It wasn't so hard when the children were little, was it?) Likewise, most kids are unaware of where the parent is coming from. However, by applying Principle Four, everyone is empowered. Both the parents and children can bring up any hidden expectations.

On the Receiving End of a Sales Pitch

Bringing up hidden expectations can quickly shift problematic situations for the better. Too often, when kids don't get their way they blame the parent. There are times when you think you are doing them a favor or doing something to help them, only to have them get even more upset than if you had done nothing. Let me give you an example of how you can make this type of interaction more positive.

I love going to garage sales. I've converted my children to them as well because they have learned that their money goes a lot farther there than at a store. A while back, I was getting

Bringing Out Hidden Expectations

ready to go for my weekly Saturday run of garage sales. My then ten-year-old daughter Emily begged for her and her friend to go with me. Knowing the potential issues I was hesitant but finally agreed and off we went. We stopped at a few sales, made a few purchases, then arrived at one that was unique.

The twenty-something "salesperson" could easily have been straight from some teen TV reality show. The first words out of her mouth were directed at these young girls: "I bet you guys would like to look sexy." She then proceeded to show them stacks of halter-tops, shorts ("short" was an understatement), crop tops, and anything else that a stripper might like. Well, these girls were drooling. The seller then turned to me and said, "You're the kind of mom who wants your girls to look cute, aren't you?" All I could hear next was, "Can I, can I?"

To everyone's disappointment, I replied that I *wasn't* that type of mom, and that I didn't want my daughter wearing this type of clothing. Immediately, *I* was the one in trouble. My daughter was embarrassed and upset. Her demeanor said that I should be punished for my inconsideration. She now had her arms folded and was mumbling angry words under her breath as she looked down at the ground.

In the past, this scenario would have ended by our going home, my daughter being angry, and me feeling guilty. But the scenario *didn't* end like that. I just brought up our exchange right there at the sale. As soon as Emily began telling me what *I* was doing wrong, I questioned her: "Who was the one who asked to come? Whose car are we driving in? Who's paying for the gas? Who purchased you the things at the other sales this morning?"

I brought up everything that I was doing and asked her why I was the one in trouble. Immediately, my daughter's attitude shifted. "Never mind," she happily remarked. "I don't need these clothes. I'm okay." We all went home much happier than if I hadn't brought up the exchange.

The success of that encounter was built on a single idea: Bringing the hidden agenda out into the light of day. Bringing it out where it can't be ignored or avoided, where responsibility must be faced. In our home, doing this has changed negative behavior to positive action. Even when an exchange seems small, it still teaches children to stay real and open, which can be very helpful later in life.

YouTube Parenting

Earlier today I went on YouTube and did a search for "parenting"—just to see what was out there. I was intrigued to find the top, featured video was one about an exchange between a fifteen-year-old girl and her father. This must have hit something of a nerve, since it had almost thirty-seven million views in less than a year!

The eight-minute video featured a father sitting in an open field, holding a printed page of a post from his daughter's Facebook wall. According to her father, she didn't think he was going to see her post, but sadly for her, he did. The father was an IT professional and was able to gain access to her profile. At

Bringing Out Hidden Expectations

first he explained that his daughter had been grounded for a few months for having previously posted something similar to the post he was now reading entitled, "To My Parents." In the posting, the daughter says that she feels as if she is her parents' slave and has to do *so* much work. The post continues, "Isn't this what you pay the housekeeper to do?" She complains that her parents suggested that she get a job instead of asking them for money; she suggests that they just pay her for all the work she does at home. The letter details the work that she is supposed to do, which she thinks leaves her no time for her own life.

In the video, the father counters each one of the complaints and expresses his side of the equation. He gives a rundown of the chores that are required of her on a daily basis and feels that these should only take a few minutes a day. He also points out that she should be responsible for her own messes just as he is responsible for his own messes. He then almost chokes when he brings up that she wants to be paid for doing her chores. He proceeds to give a run down of many of the things he provides for her such as a laptop, cords, Internet service, a cell phone, an iPod, and more, (*bringing up the exchange*). At this point, he really flips when he brings up that he spent most of the prior day upgrading her laptop (It seems as if he found the Facebook posting after he had finished doing this). So now he is going to give her a reason not to worry about her laptop in the future. You then see her laptop lying on the grass. Her father pulls out a handgun and shoots it seven times. He subsequently posts the video of this on her Facebook wall, for her and "all her friends to see."

This teen was operating with a hidden agenda. She expected to be the one to define the exchange with her parents, and thought that she had the right to judge and criticize her parents (without their knowledge) when she felt things weren't fair—yet the parents were the ones providing her with the things she wanted.

As I mentioned, there was quite a response to this video—for obvious reasons. Even Dr. Phil did a show about this on national television. I'm not saying that I think shooting the laptop was a good idea, but I do see how much of this could have been avoided if these exchanges had been brought out into the open before it escalated to all of this. I also admit that I like the idea of exchanges between parents and kids being brought out to a national audience for discussion!

Principle V

Focus on Getting the Exchange to Work, Not on Changing the Person

Focus on Getting Exchanges to Work, Not on Changing Your Child as a Person.

FOCUS your attention on
getting the exchange to work

DON'T FOCUS on "fixing" your child.

Shifting Focus

Previously, I suggested that a simple shift in focus can make a huge difference in your relationships. Parents often attempt to solve problems with a child by trying to *change* the *child*. What I would like to recommend is that you shift to changing the *exchange* with your child instead. This simple shift can profoundly transform your relationships.

For example, a mother whose children keep their rooms messy might try to make *them* be more tidy people. She might do this by preaching to them, telling them how sloppy they are or constantly reminding them what they should be doing. The mom then becomes frustrated and disappointed when her approach isn't working and her children haven't changed. Meanwhile, the children feel threatened and can become resentful. However, by focusing on getting the *exchange to work*, parents can have cleaner rooms and happier kids.

> **This simple shift can profoundly transform your relationships.**

Principle Five has helped me immensely when working with my children on a variety of issues. My burden as a mom became lighter, because, once I understood that it wasn't my job to "change" my children, I no longer needed to preach or nag. They, not me, are responsible for what they do or what they become. And they are happier because each of them is free to be his or her own best self—unhampered by concerns about my approval or disapproval. Our interactions consist mostly of developing exchanges that are mutually beneficial. It is incredible what happens. Let me give you an example…

The Ear Piercings

At my parenting seminars, parents have often asked questions like, "What age do you let your kids…?" My answer is, "It depends on the context." For example, the "rule" I observed when my daughters wanted pierced ears was, "You can get your ears pierced when you are old enough and responsible enough to take care of them." They demonstrated this to me by being responsible enough to regularly bathe, keep their hair clean, etc., *without my reminding them*. I made clear to them that trips to the doctor for infections would be on their tab—or else they would have to let their holes close. There was no predetermined "set" age.

Linda, at age fourteen, got her ears pierced without consulting me first: not a serious problem, provided she was aware of our exchange. Next she wanted more piercings, along the sides and tops of her ears in the cartilage area. I reminded her of the rule and informed her that with piercings in the cartilage area there was even a greater risk of infection than with earrings in the lobe. It is true that I did not want my daughter to have ten pierced rings in each ear, but I ignored my wants and focused on the exchange.

If I had focused on *her* (perhaps on how she would look or how others may think and judge our family) instead of on the exchange, our discussion would have turned into an argument over her appearance. My disapproval would have implied to her an unwillingness on my part to love and accept her as she is. By focusing on the exchange, I avoided all that. I refused to allow her to burden me with the consequences of an unwise decision. She knew she had full responsibility for her choice—as such, she chose to forego the additional piercings.

Always judge your *exchanges*, not your child. Even more, value the exchange first, not necessarily the child personally. By taking a step back from the emotion of the moment, you can address the bigger picture. Once the exchange has been equitably settled, then go back to your personal relationship of kindness and love. There are other times to show personal appreciation. When dealing with setting up an exchange, focus only on that. This may seem a bit impersonal, but this step of the process is crucial and beneficial in building a strong relationship between you and your child. Let me give you some more examples.

"You Said What?"

One Saturday morning, I was cleaning the house and helping Andy, who was four at the time, tidy up his toys. With his arms filled with more toys than he could possibly carry, he missed the toy box. As the toys crashed to the floor, he let out a couple of choice words that I had never heard him say before. Shocked at first, I then realized that he really had no idea what the words meant. I asked him not to use those kinds of words anymore, and he innocently replied, "Okay, Mom," and went back to picking up his toys.

After a little investigative work on my part, I realized where he had picked up his newfound vocabulary. I found the culprits in his older brother, Paul, and friends. Apparently some of Paul's friends had been using some off-color language when they visited our home to play computer games. (At the time, our household was one of the first in the neighborhood to have a computer, which we had due to a school program I was in.) Andy happened to be around and overheard them. Wanting to act like the big boys, he was mimicking them.

I later discussed this with Paul, offered him an exchange, and clarified the rules of the exchange: "You can use my computer, if you guys don't use that kind of language when your little brother is around. You're teaching Andy how to swear and he thinks it's a really cool thing to do. So by you having your friends over, *I'm* having to clean up Andy's vocabulary. Either the swearing stops, or you guys can't use my computer."

I didn't have to fight with Paul or get on his case about being a bad example or having terrible friends. I focused on the exchange. Guess what? It worked. Paul took the responsibility for correcting the problem and explained the new conditions to his friends—I didn't have to. At first, Paul was embarrassed to tell his friends not to swear when his younger brother was around. But wanting to use the computer, especially with his friends, was more important to Paul, so he followed through. Andy's language soon reverted back to that of a four-year-old. The situation was easily resolved, without me becoming angry at or critical of Paul.

The Art of *Warcraft*

A couple of years ago, I had been out running errands for most of the day. As I was driving home, it dawned on me that my car was really dirty and that I wanted it to be clean before I met with friends that evening for dinner. I realized that when I arrived home I would only have about twenty minutes to take a quick shower and change. I wouldn't have time to both get ready and wash my car.

I phoned my teenage son, Andy, who had been playing *World of Warcraft*, an online computer game, when I left that morning. These games can go on for hours or even days, so I was not surprised to learn that he was still playing. When I asked, he admitted that he hadn't done the chores he'd agreed to. So, I figured this was a good time for an exchange.

"Andy, I need you to wash my car for me in a few minutes," I explained. "I will only be there long enough to take a quick shower and change. Since you haven't done your work today, I need you to do this favor for me."

"I can't mom," he insisted. "I'm in the middle of my game. I won't be able to help you until later." Again I explained that I needed it done within the next few minutes. "If you don't want to help me right now, that's fine, just remember whose computer, Internet service, and electricity you're using." That was all I said.

I went home, took my shower, got ready, said bye to Andy and left (not knowing if he had washed the car for me or not). Again, not to my surprise, he *had* washed the car while I was getting ready. He knew that there was an equitable exchange happening between us: his using my things for most of the day in exchange for quickly washing my car. I called him from the road to thank him for washing the car. "No problem mom. Have a fun time."

I have talked to and known many parents over the years who, in similar situations, made the mistake of focusing directly on their kids (not the exchange) and never resolved a thing. By merely reminding your kids of your expectations within exchanges (focusing on the exchange, not the person) you can solve many problems. I didn't get on Andy's case for being on the computer all day. I just reminded him that part of the cost of his using my things was helping me when I needed it.

Equitable Exchanges

A while back, I was at lunch with one of my sisters when the conversation turned to children and then to her eighteen-year-old son, Jacob. Jacob was a good kid. He volunteered his time with church activities, helped anyone in need, and attended the local community college. He also prided himself on playing in a rock band. The struggle she was having was that Jacob never did any work around the house. She had asked him to help, but he ignored her. Finally she arrived at the point of saying, "If you will just put your dirty clothes in the hamper, I'll wash them for you." "No can do!" was his reply as he hurried out the door. Eventually she pinned him down to find out what was going on. He enlightened her: "Now that I'm eighteen, I don't need to help anymore. Besides, I play in a rock band, and I'm too busy with more important things."

These were Jacob's hidden expectations. Since he had become an "adult," he believed that he didn't need to help anymore (at least not at home). He was now so important that *his* time was more valuable than that of his mother, who worked full time and had four other children at home. Jacob was involved in great work. He was helping so many people that he didn't have time to help in his own home. Now that my sister understood what his unspoken expectations were, she began to deal with Jacob in a real way, and not in his world of illusion. She began to set up equitable exchanges regardless of his age or commitments. As a result, the relationship changed for the positive and Jacob carried his portion of the responsibilities of living at home.

Just as in a business relationship, your child makes exchanges with you to get what she wants and needs. You, as a parent, need to ensure the exchanges with your child are equitable, just as a business owner finds that proper balance of fairness with his customers—one in which they keep coming back and he still makes a profit.

Cost/Benefit Analysis

Getting a full time job after going off of welfare allowed me, for the first time in a while, to buy nice things for my children. Juliana, who was sixteen at the time, was especially pleased with the name brand shoes I purchased for her. For me, though, my combined responsibilities as single mother and breadwinner were overwhelming. It felt as if the children's help around the house was diminishing while the burden on me was becoming greater.

> **You, as a parent, need to ensure the exchanges with your child are equitable.**

As I recognized that our exchanges were becoming less equitable, I knew that I needed to reset our exchange. I gathered the children together to discuss what was going on. I explained to them that I needed more help with the housework now that my outside work had increased. I needed them to carry their part of the responsibilities without me having to continually remind them.

I could see that the children were somewhat upset by me telling them this, especially Juliana, who was now in tears. Crying, she pleaded, "We shouldn't have to do more housework just because *you* decided to go to work." (That was her hidden expectation.) I then asked where she thought the money came from to buy the nice shoes she was wearing. I then added, "I guess I could cut back on my hours so I'll have more time to do housework, but if I do, no more name brand shoes."

Juliana's entire demeanor shifted as she comprehended that there was a cost to having the shoes she liked. She now knew that she should play a part in paying that cost by being involved in the exchange. She agreed to help around the house and was happy to do so. By again focusing and resetting the exchange, my problem solved positively, without negative words aimed at my kids. There was no judgment that my daughter wanted to wear name brand clothes. This process works because it increases your child's awareness of costs: they share in those costs and learn to be more responsible for the benefits.

Exchanges can be made regardless of your financial status. I used to buy my kids' favorite foods with food stamps and make them meals they enjoyed in exchange for baby-sitting help. I've exchanged playing board games with them for help folding clothes. Parents with a lot of money shouldn't "owe" more to their children than anyone else. Parents should use whatever means they have available to help their child make rewarding exchanges. Use what you have to help them learn accountability and responsibility, and then see the relationship between costs and benefits in your exchanges.

Wrestling with Wrestling

While in middle school, my daughter Emily was a World Wrestling Federation fan. I was not, but that was okay. I allowed her to have her choices if they were not harmful to her, and if others didn't have to pay a cost because of them. But I did require an exchange when she wanted to watch wrestling on a TV that I had bought, or view cable channels that I paid for, or use *my* Internet access. The exchange I required was that she not become isolated in the world of wrestling (which she had been for a while until the exchange was brought up) and that she must interact with the family and with me in order (for her) to use these things. Once the exchange was worked out, she totally agreed and it worked out great!

> **Awareness is the key.**

Parents reading this may already be functioning in a similar way. I have parents tell me at seminars that this is really nothing new. The difference is that they are now more aware of what they are doing, and they can help their children become more aware as well. Awareness is the key—it's what builds responsibility. This next story will show how your child can take responsibility for what he wants, instead of being upset that he doesn't get everything his way.

Long Showers

When she was in high school, my daughter Juliana loved to take long showers in the morning before school. The problem wasn't that she wanted to take long showers; the problem was that there were eight of us in the house and only one bathroom.

The rest of the family was complaining to me that they didn't have access to the bathroom at a crucial time in the morning.

My first inclination was to scold her for being selfish and inconsiderate. But by staying with the exchange rule of not focusing on the person—just the exchange—I put the responsibility on her to come up with a solution. She did. Since the shower curtain was not see-through, she agreed to leave the bathroom door unlocked so the family could use the bathroom while she was in the shower. This worked out great and everyone got what they needed. I know, since I have five daughters, that this wasn't an easy choice for a sixteen-year-old girl to make, but it gave her what she wanted.

The preceding stories should illustrate the fifth principle of focusing on a working exchange, not on wanting to change who the other person is or what they want within the exchange. This is a valuable key that can help promote a more trusting relationship between parents and their children. I know that, for me, this was a pivotal step to my family's transformation.

Review: The Five Principles

1. All relationships are exchanges.

2. Exchanges are run by expectations.

3. Some expectations running exchanges are hidden.

4. Bringing the hidden expectations "out-on-the-table" changes the exchange.

5. Focus on getting the exchange to work, not on changing the other person.

All relationships are based on exchanges, whether you are aware of it or not. Using this approach, you don't try to control your child. All you need to do is control *your part of the exchange*, for everyone's benefit. This new kind of relationship between you and your child is what I call an "exchange-based approach."

An exchange-based approach for working with your child can eliminate emotional power struggles. You can negotiate exchanges that work for everyone involved by consciously focusing on getting each exchange to work best.

Be sure to memorize or write down these principles so you can use them each day in your parenting relationships and experience the remarkable results.

Section Three

Making the Change

Parenting with Benefits

At this point, I have given you a five-step exchange process to use when interacting with your child—a valuable tool. Imagine you are a carpenter and you have been hired to build a house. You arrive at the location where the house is to be built and the contractor instructs you to get started. You think you are ready, but then you realize that there are no tools for you to work with. How grateful would you be if you *only had a hammer*? That is how I see this process. It is a tool that helps you get the job done—just as a hammer would if you were building a house.

Now that all seven of my children are adults, I can look back and see how beneficial this tool--the tool of exchange--has been in our lives. At first I used it out of pure necessity. I needed a way to get my children to take more responsibility for themselves while taking some of the weight off of my shoulders. I now recognize that what I "stumbled upon" was much more than just a quick fix for my problems at that time. This process has proven to be effective not only as a household management tool but in amazing ways that I never expected.

I like to refer to these benefits as *by-products* of the process. A by-product is a secondary, unintended result. I implemented the exchanges with my children to help them have a better chance at successful lives. The "unintended" result was happier, more responsible, more confident and loving children. Who knew?

In my first parenting book, *A Little Secret for Dealing with Teens,* the "secret" I was referring to was these unintended, magical results. We were able to easily resolve situations *and* improve our relationships, despite the difficult circumstances that we were faced with. I watched my children take responsibility instead of getting angry. Win-win all the way around!

Parenting Benefits

Let me share with you in a little more detail the other benefits, or *by-products,* that I discovered while implementing this process.

Benefit: *Increased mutual respect.* One of the most rewarding changes that I have seen in my children is the increased respect they have not only for me, but for each other. Once they became more aware of how each person pays a price for what he or she needs and gets, my children made more of an effort to help each other and had more consideration for one another. They continually showed gratitude for the things I did for them because they knew that I didn't *have* to do it for them. Awareness makes such a difference!

If you think about it, aren't people generally nicer to you (or in the business world, willing to give you money) if you have something that they want? If someone has something you want, you certainly don't deliberately offend them, do you? This is

Putting it All Together

what happened in our home. Everyone wanted our family to do well, and everyone became aware of their own role.

At times, raising children can be like trying to row across a big lake with the entire family in a boat. Everyone needs to work together to get to the other side. I know some kids who might jump up and down in heels in the boat because they were angry about having to help. They don't realize that if they do this, they sink themselves and everybody else. Both children and parents need to continually recognize that the family is in the boat together. By rowing in unison, everyone can safely make it to the other side.

> **As kids become aware of the cost of their actions and the exchanges, they will be less inclined to be irresponsible.**

Benefit: *Increased self-esteem.* What child wouldn't benefit from an increase in self-esteem? As your children become involved in working exchanges, they feel a sense of accomplishment. Throughout the exchanges, my children became more confident about their choices and themselves.

Recently, there has been a lot of discussion in the media about children taking more responsibility for themselves and their actions. Parents often take responsibility for their children's actions when what they need to do is help their children take responsibility for what they do. As kids become aware of the cost of their actions and the exchanges, they will be less inclined to be irresponsible.

The Parenting Exchange

Responsibility becomes an everyday reality instead of a nebulous concept that adults talk about.

Benefit: *Gratitude, not entitlement.* "Entitlement" seems to be a popular buzzword lately. When children take responsibility for themselves, they no longer feel entitled.

Several years ago, while my children were still at home, my work required that I put in many hours of overtime. As a result, my kids needed to help more with cooking and watching the younger children. When payday came, I announced, "Let's go shopping for summer clothes, now that it's getting hotter." We went shopping and I purchased each of the kids one or two items that they needed. As soon as the purchases were made, I was bombarded with thanks. I must have heard over thirty "thank-yous." *Then* I brought up the exchange that allowed me to take them shopping. "The reason I can buy you these clothes," I explained, "is because I have been working overtime. The reason I could work overtime is because you all helped at home to do the work I would normally do. By you helping me, I can help you."

It is important that you, as the parent, verbalize your exchanges so your child recognizes that there is an exchange involved. By doing this, you create a sense of value and respect within your relationships. With everyone aware of how this exchange worked, my children knew that there was a cost to what they were getting. They didn't just demand I buy them clothes because I'm the mom. They were grateful that I worked extra so they could have clothes that they liked. When

Putting it All Together

you create an awareness of the process, your child becomes more mindful and appreciative.

Benefit: *A lighter load on you.* I don't know one parent who doesn't want their load lightened. Raising kids is difficult work. When I was in school full time and carrying a tremendous load, I realized that my children were the only ones around to help me lighten it. So I shifted many of my day-to-day tasks over to them. Through that experience, I learned about this valuable tool—exchanges—that can help any parent. Knowing that their children are actively helping resolve problems offers overloaded parents considerable relief.

As you implement the exchange system, you will experience your own rewarding *by-products.* You will be able to create new and beneficial exchanges unique to you and your family, as well as find innovative ways to effectively and beneficially use this system.

Making the Shift

Shifting to an exchange-based approach requires two key elements:

1) **Commitment**
2) **Paying the "cost"**

Commitment

Have you ever had a bit of insomnia and flipped on the TV in the middle of the night? If so, you've surely seen an abundance of infomercials for fitness gadgets and diet regimes that claim magical solutions while touting their life-changing benefits. You may have even called that toll free number flashing on the screen and ordered whatever it was, hoping it would be half as effective as promised by the physicians and fitness experts who testified in the infomercial. Whenever I see these, I think to myself, "If these programs really are as easy and effective as they claim, why don't more people lose weight? Why is there an obesity epidemic in our country?"

> **Your success will depend on how committed you are to applying these concepts and sticking with them.**

Part of the answer, I concluded, is that there are costs associated with losing weight and getting in shape that many

Putting it All Together

aren't willing to pay. For example, you can only eat certain foods or you have to exercise regularly. So why don't most people stick with their plan of action? I suspect it's because they don't want to make the necessary sacrifices.

Weight loss is a fitting metaphor for improving your relationship with your child. Your success will depend on how committed you are to applying these concepts and sticking with them.

The sacrifices you might have to make as a parent include:

- Letting go of pre-conceived ideas on parenting
- Letting go of control
- Letting go of how others may judge your parenting style
- Allowing your children to experience the consequences of their actions

Just like a weight loss plan, an exchange-based approach to parenting may be easier for some than for others. The more committed you are, the more likely you will be to follow through and see results.

Paying the Cost

If a ball is rolling in one direction, a certain amount of energy must be applied to that ball to move it in a different direction. It is a law of physics, and it is a law of kids. I remember one time when our family needed to move to a new location. My older kids dragged their feet, whined, complained loudly, and tried to convince me not to move. Regardless of the kicking and screaming, we moved. After we had lived at our new place for a time, I heard these same complainers say, "I really like where we live now a lot better than where we used to live." Change requires sacrifice. That's why everyone resists change, even if the change is later beneficial.

Changing your relationship with your child to one based on exchanges will extract a cost. As a parent, the promise of a happier, more productive family may be enough to entice you to give this process a try, but these rewards might not be so alluring to your child. Attachment to the status quo can be very strong. Keep in mind that your future benefits will far outweigh your current costs.

One Mom Who Paid the Cost

A friend of mine, Sarah, shared with me her story of paying the cost. Sarah's family was in the habit of ignoring her and any efforts she made to help them. She would cook, clean, and do laundry while the rest of the family watched television or played with friends. Eventually, she woke up to how bad things had become. She decided that it was time to have more equitable exchanges. Sarah attempted to work out a plan with the family to help her with the housework, but to no avail. (Why would they change if they were happy with the status quo?) When it became evident to Sarah that she was acting alone in this exchange and nothing was changing, she simply stopped doing *everything*.

Putting it All Together

The laundry piled up to the ceiling, the dishes were headed in the same direction, and the family started having hunger pangs. Her kids and husband cried and pleaded. Sarah held her ground and did nothing. Her family tried every strategy they could think of to get her back into old ways (except to help her), but she wouldn't give in.

Finally, after two weeks of soiled clothes, dirty dishes, a chaotic household, and—especially—the empty stomachs, the family capitulated. An exchange was worked out where everyone in the house did his or her share. No one member had to carry the entire load. Once a routine was established, everyone was glad to have things working again. What was also great was the increased value and respect that each member of the family gained for each other as they shared in this exchange.

Sarah's strike wasn't easy, but it worked. In the future, if the work began to slack off, just the threat of another strike moved her family back into action. This was the price this mother had to pay to have a more equitable exchange with her family. She paid the cost, and having done so, she secured an equitable exchange that benefited the entire family.

The Parenting Exchange

Parental Accountability

For the process of the *parenting exchange* to really work its magic, the parent must maintain a moral accountability to the truth *and* the highest well being for their child. Denying the *real* agenda he or she imposes can be very dangerous to the parent-child relationship. An exchange-based approach only works from the top down: from management to employee; from parents to children. It doesn't work from the bottom up. Parents are naturally in a power position. The parent is the one providing the wisdom and financial support for the children. If a child sees that a parent is being unfair in the exchange or that he or she is not being truthful and the parent hides his or her real intent, the child will be frustrated and feel powerless to change things and often will become angry. This will cause the relationship to be inequitable and not work. On the other hand, if a child is not being honest, the parent can deal with it and fix it because of the parent's position.

> **The parent must maintain a moral accountability to the truth *and* the highest well being for their child.**

One time I was working with a struggling teen and his mother. The teenager was trying to express what the problem was between the two of them. He haltingly explained how his mother contradicts him in most situations. I had to chuckle to myself when the mother immediately replied that this wasn't true. As

Putting it All Together

she was contradicting her son, she was proving him to be correct.

What was this teen to do? He was not in a position to change things and could not feel safe talking about his mom's expectations or agenda. He was stuck. This is why a hidden expectation or agenda, especially coming from a parent, can be so detrimental to furthering any worthwhile change.

Let me share with you a true story of someone I know. You will see how important it is (especially for your child's wellbeing) for the exchange to be transparent for both the parent and the child.

Karin was a wife and mother with a large family. Besides this, she constantly seemed to have some kind of an important "quest" in her life. She liked being a community leader and helping others. While never discussing it with them, she expected her family to support her in these pursuits. When she left to speak or meet with people, she just took for granted that her family should assume her responsibilities at home. Her family was confused because there was never any specific cause Karin was dedicated to; she just seemed to be gone a lot. For several years, when Karin would go out and about, most of the load fell on her oldest teenage daughter, Brittney.

Brittney was very reliable, always tending to the kids, cooking for the family, and doing other things she felt her mom should do. During her mother's frequent absences from home, Brittney was overwhelmed by all the responsibility. Karin tried to explain to her daughter: "I need your help because what I am doing is so important, and this how you can support me."

The Parenting Exchange

But Brittney never agreed to this exchange; her mother imposed it on her. Brittney had almost no free time, and even her schoolwork was affected. During the time that Brittney should have been learning, having fun, and doing things with her friends, she was expected to be a "mom" instead. This situation went on for a few years.

Finally one day, Brittney had had enough and her family found that she was gone. She had eloped with her first real boyfriend, a boy her mother didn't even know existed. Brittney wrote her mother a note, packed her bags, and left.

The next week, I was at a meeting where Karin was crying to a group of women as she told them about Brittney. "After all I've done for her," she lamented, "this is all the thanks I get. Now I'm going to have to watch the children by myself." Tears were streaming down her face.

Karin had a one-sided exchange with Brittney—one in which her daughter wasn't a participant. Brittney believed that she had no choice in it and received almost nothing in return. Karin liked talking about having a large family, but she didn't like the responsibility that went with it. Karin used guilt and parental pressure to get her daughter to do her job. There was never any honest discussion between the two of them to work out an equitable exchange. Finally, when Brittney had had enough—she left.

If you want exchanges to benefit all those involved, being honest (especially with yourself) is your *only* choice. If you expect this approach to work, neither you nor your children can lie. As the parent, you must be willing to give up whatever

Putting it All Together

hidden agendas you have in your relationship with your child. Put everything out on the table. Your goal is to create an atmosphere of equity in which everyone clearly understands the rules. Without honesty, success is impossible. Parents need to take responsibility for what they impose and not deny their true agendas.

The Parenting Exchange

Section Four

Living the Exchange

Putting it All Together

The *parenting exchange* is an interactive process. What started out for me as a survival strategy became something better—a strategy for thriving! While some parents *demand* respect from their children, I used this exchange process to create genuine mutual respect without ever having to ask for it.

This is a results-driven approach. By applying and actively living these principles, you can attain the results you desire. For the remainder of this book, I will be sharing stories, scenarios, thoughts, principles, and experiences that demonstrate how this can be accomplished. Some of these are my experiences while others are stories I have heard along the way. I hope this will provide you with an overall picture of how to integrate the *parenting exchange* into your everyday parenting.

As you will see, you can begin using these principles at a very young age with your child. Of course, how you apply these principles with a small child will certainly be different from how you apply them with a teen. I found that with my children I was able to make adjustments in our relationships as the situations allowed. I also found that the older my children got, the more interactive the process became. This helped to prepare them to become more aware and independent adults. As a mother, I really couldn't ask for more.

You are in Charge

One of the requisites to success in this process is honesty. As a parent, you are in the "power" position. You make the money. You own (rent) the home. You have the knowledge and wisdom. If you misuse this leverage, this process won't work. In fact, it will have the opposite effect.

I have known parents who have good intentions in their relationships with their children but who feel as if they have lost control—feeling as if they are going the wrong way on a one-way street, with their kid at the wheel. Often the parents watch their children act in irresponsible and inequitable ways, without slowing down to see who is really "driving."

> **Remember, you are the one who paid the cost to get where you are today--not your child.**

This exchange-based approach, however, helps parents take back the wheel and regain control. Instead of dictating to their children, parents can instead use their personal resources (time, property, etc.) for mutual benefit. This natural power, used wisely, eliminates power struggles and focuses attention on

Putting it All Together

getting exchanges to work. Remember, you are the one who paid the cost to get where you are today--not your child.

In the business world, an effective manager would never let employees with little or no experience dictate how the company is run. The reason employees are generally willing to do as they are asked is because they are positively compensated for their efforts. All parties have agreed to a mutually beneficial exchange, with management in charge. This same approach can be used within your family. The parent typically has something that their child wants, such as time, assistance, computer, money, a car, etc. This puts parents in the power position, able to make exchanges with their children, not always necessarily vice versa.

Two-year-old running the show

A while back, my stepdaughter and son-in-law came to stay with our family for a few days. Before they left, they needed to do some shopping for their trip home. Four adults and two-year-old Seth set out for the store. As we entered, the parents allowed Seth to lead the way. At first, Seth refused to ride in the cart; he wanted to walk. Then he noticed a drink stand off to his right, and of course, he wanted a drink. His mother attempted a deal with him: "You can have the drink if you ride in the cart." The deal fell through. Now we had a tot walking even slower, alternating between a suck on his straw and a step ahead. So, here were the adults, all bent over and staring at the drink cup as it teetered on the edge of disaster—slowly walking through the store behind our two-year-old leader.

Eventually, the parents found the aisle they were looking for. The toddler put the unfinished drink down in the middle of the aisle and decided to rearrange the neatly stacked shelves nearby. As his mom grabbed the stuff to put it back, Seth ran to another display. Then it was his dad's turn to pick things up. Then all four of us were helping. If we took anything away from him, he screamed. All of our attention was centered on him. In the middle of this chaos, it dawned on me what was going on. We were letting a two-year-old dictate the schedule and behavior of four adults!

After all was said and done, it took almost an hour to buy something that should have taken five minutes. This is a silly, but *typical*, story. Parents allow behavior like this all the time. We let kids set our agenda for us. We relinquish our power to our children more often than we might recognize.

Reality TV: Looking for Answers

I recall a reality show a few years back that focused on parenting issues. One particular episode featured a mother and her two teenaged daughters. The show opened as the mother explained what she wanted from her girls was for them to grow up to be confident and self-assured. She shared that, up to this point, she had mistakenly allowed them to always make their own decisions (believing that this would teach them to be responsible). When the show aired, her girls were totally out of

Putting it All Together

control (that's why they were being featured on the show). They had become demanding of their mother, yet at the same time, they seemed to be anything but confident.

This mother was at her wit's end, looking for answers. I *did* understand this mom's desire to teach her girls to be decision-makers. However, she needed to retain the control of the exchanges with her daughters by not allowing *them* to be in the driver's seat.

So, how can a parent do things differently using this exchange process? How do you teach and interact with your child by implementing these new rules of the exchange?

In the case of our two-year-old shopper, here's how it would have gone down if I had been the mom. First, I would have asked him if he wanted to go into the store with everyone else. (As an aside, I have discovered that most small children can understand "grown-ups" at a much earlier age than I ever thought possible. After raising my kids, I know that they do understand quite a bit at this age.) By asking your child, you are giving him the opportunity to enter into this exchange. This step of the process then puts you in the driver's seat, so to speak.

Now you can set the parameters. If the child doesn't agree, then you end the exchange (when possible). Then the child begins to learn that he needs to be responsible for his end of the exchange. If the child wanted to go, I would have explained to him that he would need to ride happily in the cart while we were in the store. As soon as the whining started, I would have calmly asked him to stop and if not, we would go wait in the car outside. If the whining kept going, I would have immediately taken him to the car (calmly with no discussion) and waited until everyone else came out. Other than spending some last minute family time together, there really wasn't a reason to have four adults in the store anyway. This action would begin to teach this child, at a young age, that he isn't the one setting the exchange.

There is a price for a parent to pay initially in order to prevent future problems. But it would have been easier to pay the cost of sitting in the car with this toddler than to have him believe he is in charge of the entire shopping adventure.

You Can "Exchange" at Any Age

When I was promoting my first parenting book, a book for parents of teens, parents told me they wished they could use my process but didn't feel that it applied to their young children. Actually this exchange system can be used with children of any age. Here are some stories and experiences to exemplify this and help you gain a clearer picture of how to integrate this process at any stage of your child's life.

Computers and Diapers

Speaking as a mother of seven, I will tell you that there are a few parenting duties that never get easier no matter how many children you have. One of those is potty-training. It is *no* fun! When it came time for this task with my last child, I have

Putting it All Together

to admit, I procrastinated. Eventually, though, it had to be done. Unfortunately for me, this came during a time when my plate was overflowing—while I was a single mother and full-time student and trying to turn my family life around.

Also during this time, I acquired my first computer. One of the government assistance programs that I was in provided me with one. Being that this was in the mid-nineties, this was not only our family's first computer but the first in our small community as well. My kids found it a great resource for playing games—especially my youngest, Andy, who was almost three and still not potty trained.

During the limited time I had to spend with my children, getting Andy out of diapers became a top priority. After attempting the tried (and not so true) methods of cheering him on, including group applause from the whole family following intermittent success, he continued to not take responsibility for going to the potty. I began to notice that the times he *really* didn't take that responsibility was when he was on the computer. He would get into game mode (his favorite was called Bailey's Book House) and not want to get up.

I recognized that this would be a good opportunity to help Andy become more aware of exchanges as well as get him potty trained. So, he and I had a conversation, the best possible with an almost-three-year-old, which went something like this:

"Andy, I see that you really like playing on the computer."

He nods

"But Andy, I'm still having to put diapers on you because you won't go to the potty."

The Parenting Exchange

He nods again.

"Do you see anyone else wearing diapers that is using the computer?"

He shakes his head and says, "no."

"Well, did you know that only big boys and girls that go potty and don't wear diapers can use the computer?"

He looks at me.

"Since this is the rule, that only big people that don't wear diapers can use the computer, you won't be able to use it until you learn to go potty, ok?"

"Ok."

Two days later: potty training done.

Once he realized that he needed to take responsibility for himself to be able to use what I was providing for him, he did just that. I figured if he had the capacity to understand the games, he had the capacity to understand our exchange—and he did.

Infant Exchange

Now that I have grandchildren, I continue to use these principles with them. When I was writing the manuscript for my first book, I was under a tight deadline to get it to the publisher. I needed to make effective use of almost every minute. During this time, one of my stepsons and his wife came to visit us in southern California with their three children, including Emma, who was only about 7 months old. During their stay, the family wanted to go to Disneyland but didn't

Putting it All Together

think it would be wise to take Emma with them. Knowing how much they really wanted to go, I offered to watch her while the family went.

The next morning the family ate breakfast and left for a day of adventure. I was left at home to keep writing and watch Emma. Once Emma realized her parents were gone, she clung to me like *I* was her mom. I wanted to hold and play with her all day, but I needed to get some writing done as well.

So, before I began to write, I set out to ensure that her needs would be met. She was fed and her diaper changed, and all was well. It wasn't time for a nap yet, so I placed several toys and her favorite blanket on the floor next to where I would be writing. Predictably, as soon as I set her down, she began to cry and hold her arms up for me to pick her up.

I knew right then that I needed to shift this "exchange." I sensed that her expectation of the exchange was that she would stop crying if I picked her up. So, I looked lovingly at her and explained, "Emma, I will be sitting right here," pointing to my chair, "and you will be right here," pointing to her blanket. "Look, here are your toys and your blanket. I'm not going anywhere, just here in this chair (again patting the chair). You can play and even touch my leg. Play with your toys and everything is fine." I used many hand gestures as well as a kind, calming voice. I could see her taking all of this in. Once she was convinced that everything would be ok, she sat on her blanket, right next to me, and enjoyed playing with some new toys.

Somehow she understood that everything would be fine without me having to hold her. (I'm thinking that some of her

The Parenting Exchange

thinking in this exchange was that she only felt safe when I was holding her.) By me doing what I could to communicate what I wanted from her, we both had a calm and productive day.

As I have integrated this process over the years and with children at all ages, I have been able to recognize more of why we had the results that we did. For example, one of the "by-products" was the increase in them taking responsibility for getting what they wanted. They discovered that it required an effort on their part to initiate an exchange when they wanted something from me (or others). The older they got, the more responsible they became for getting this. Most kids (unconsciously) leave it to the parent to define the exchanges. Once your child realizes that it is his or her responsibility to figure this out, it's fun to see them work out the exchange.

> **Once your child realizes that it is his or her responsibility to figure this out, it's fun to see them work out the exchange.**

When my oldest daughter, Juliana, was in high school, she was on the golf team. One evening, while I was busy getting my two preschoolers ready for bed (and doing twenty other things), I looked over to the kitchen and saw Juliana washing dishes and cleaning. Smiling to myself, I sensed that she needed something from me. Sure enough, when she finished cleaning the kitchen, she approached me and asked, "Mom, can you take me to school tomorrow morning? I have golf practice and don't want to take my golf clubs on the bus" (she later told me it embarrassed her). "Since I cleaned the kitchen, you will have extra time in the morning to take me," she reasoned. Of course I agreed, especially since it gave me more time to help her. The really great thing about all of this is that not only did I not have to argue with my sixteen-year-old daughter about helping me, I never even had to ask!

When your child comes to you asking for something, you may want to respond with questions like: "If I do this for you, what do I get in return?" Or, "No offense, but why should I?" These questions may seem a little strong, but the alternative is having your child remain unaware of the costs of your exchange or taking advantage of you. Once the exchange-based pattern is established in your family, you will see your child approach you with exchange—instead of just a request or even a demand—while developing into more responsible adults.

Skills for the "Real World"

It seems as if kids now have more "skills" than ever. I know that I have asked my children from time to time to help me figure out how to work a computer program or configure a jumble of cords and plugs when setting up new video equipment. I'll admit that I also needed assistance from them when learning how to "tweet." What all of this tells me is that when our kids want to learn something, they do. But when they don't, they tend to either put it off or just not do it. I've also learned that

The Parenting Exchange

they will certainly let you do as many things on their behalf as you offer to do.

My very first full-time job was working for a few months at the Department of Motor Vehicles. Through my position there, I was privy to a couple of interesting scenarios involving young people.

The first one occurred when a consumer economics teacher at the local high school gave the students in his classes an assignment: How would they spend a million dollars in thirty days? Of course, many of his students decided they would buy expensive cars such as BMWs or Mercedes-Benzes. For the assignment, they needed information on the costs of registering and licensing such cars. Our DMV office fielded more than fifty phone calls in two weeks from people requesting such information. Of all the calls, only one was from an actual student. The rest of the calls were from parents who were doing their children's schoolwork for them.

> **Parents should expect, especially as they become older, that the kids themselves carry their respective "loads."**

The second scenario happened when a young woman came to my window in tears. She asked me if she could return her personalized license plates and get a refund. When I asked her what the reason was, she replied, "When I turned 18, my parents limited the amount of money they gave me to live on each month. Before this, my parents gave me everything I wanted with no restrictions. I had no idea what anything cost or how to budget. So, when I decided on the license plates for my car, I bought custom ones. I now understand that I can't afford these," she confessed, holding back tears. "I really need my money back."

My heart definitely went out to her, but the system wouldn't allow for a refund. I had to inform her that she could only get regular plates when the year expired.

In both of these situations, the parents of these young adults taught them that they didn't need to be accountable for what should have been their personal responsibilities. The parents would give them, buy for them, call for them, and I'm assuming even more.

Parents should expect, especially as their kids become older, that the kids themselves carry their respective "loads." For many reasons, such as guilt or wanting the best for their children, parents may be denying those they love the experiences that would make them stronger. The *parenting exchange* process can support your child in taking responsibility for her wants and needs by handing off the responsibility as soon as she is capable of shouldering it.

My Daughter's Friend and Her "Need" for WIC

Before moving on, I just have to share with you the following story of an "entitled" friend of my daughter. Juliana shared this with me one day while we were at the store, so I asked her to send it my way to add to my book. And, as Juliana says, "The names have been changed to protect the crazies."

The Parenting Exchange

Juliana has a dear friend named "Abby" who has a great heart and loves her dog way too much. She—unfortunately or fortunately, depending on how you look at it—was raised in a very privileged silver-spoon upbringing. Her dad is a doctor and has given her a life of ease. She still receives a monthly allowance, even though she is well into her twenties, lives in another state, and has her own job.

One night Abby went to Wal-Mart to buy a few items for her dog. One would imagine that she would go to the pet section to buy these items, but not Abby. She fed her dog only the finest (non-pet) milk and cereal, as well as baby food out of a jar. At the checkout line, the cashier gave her the total, and Abby realized that her allowance was running a little short that month. She only had a twenty-dollar bill with her, which wasn't enough for her purchases. She told the cashier that she needed to put back a few of the items. Feeling what you can only imagine was concern and worry for a baby going without food, the helpful cashier informed Abby that there was a program called WIC which would allow her to get all of these items for free. "What?" Abby cried, "I can get this stuff for free? Well, sign me up!" The cashier gave her more information about the program and where she could go to apply. I'm sure that the cashier was so happy to have helped out a "mother" in need of milk and baby food.

I wish at this point that I could have been a fly on the wall or at least a nosy customer in the checkout behind her, because the cashier then asked Abby, "So how old is your baby?"

"*Baby*? I don't have a baby. This stuff is for my dog!"

Putting it All Together

Having been on the WIC program for many years (if you are unfamiliar with this program, it is a government food supplementation program focused on nutrition for women, infants, and children), I understand how the cashier would have felt helping out this young "mother." However, this entitled young woman didn't have a clue about this world she had not been exposed to.

I believe that until our kids have left the nest, we owe it to them to hand more and more responsibility back over to them. By doing this, we can help to increase their life skills in multiple ways.

A Dynamic Process

Looking back at my many decades of parenting, I will admit that if someone had had a secret camera in our home, for the most part anyone watching might have thought that I was somewhat of a "lazy" mom. Not in the sense that I wasn't a hard worker and just sat around all day watching soap operas and eating bonbons, but in the sense that the amount of time and effort I used to directly "parent" was minimal. The idea of "helicopter" parenting is incomprehensible to me. "Why would I expend energy for something that another person is capable of doing for himself?"

I remember times when I would be in front of my house visiting with some of the other neighborhood parents. They would ask me how one of my children was doing on a particular homework assignment or report. I was embarrassed

The Parenting Exchange

to admit that I had no idea. That was my kids' homework, not mine.

I had plenty on my plate with a houseful of children, even while I was married. This substantially increased when I became a single parent. So, as I was looking for answers, I knew that my parenting solutions needed to be not only beneficial, but fit seamlessly into my family's daily life.

The exchanges in my parenting provided me with valuable options that enabled me to become a more effective parent, while at the same time relieving me of a substantial load. Here is how:

- These exchanges take place *within* the existing relationship.
- It is a model-based approach where you "plug-in" your concern right into the steps.
- It is an on-going, interactive, relational process between you and your child.
- It is an approach that doesn't require the memorization of rules or needing to know what to do when.
- It is a method that flourishes with honesty, integrity, and consistency on the part of the parent, which should be the basis of any meaningful parenting relationship.
- This methodology is dynamic and takes place in the moment, consequently helping to keep relationships real.

Putting it All Together

- It is fluid and provides the flexibility that is uniquely required in this fast-paced, high-tech world that you and your child interact in.

A Dynamic Process

As I just mentioned, if you have children, you know how dynamic and fast-moving their world is—nothing stays the same. Your life becomes much easier when you can adapt the exchanges within your and your children's changing world. I have a general guideline that says we can always change the exchange. Of course, terms of exchanges shouldn't be arbitrarily changed on a parent's whim. When changes need to be made, let all of those affected know why change is necessary and how it will benefit everyone.

> **When changes need to be made, let all of those affected know why change is necessary and how it will benefit everyone.**

If you have more than one child, this means being flexible in how you uniquely exchange with each child. And as you exchange with each child individually, consider carefully what to do in each situation. The exchange should be based on what will be best for each child, not just on what you *can* or want to do.

Robert, a friend of mine, excitedly purchased his son Matt a used car on his sixteenth birthday and offered to maintain it for him as well. As the months passed, Robert could see that this exchange wasn't working well. As the novelty wore off, he

The Parenting Exchange

began to realize how much this was costing him. He had purchased the vehicle, and now he continued to pay for gas and repairs. The insurance was about to bankrupt him.

Robert began to comprehend that this exchange was pretty one-sided, and that his son wasn't doing anything in return for all that he had done and was still doing for him. It was easy to see that Matt held a sense of entitlement, which wasn't benefiting either of them.

After I shared with Robert these principles of exchange, he decided to shift his exchange with Matt. So he sat down with his son and notified him that from that time forward, he would no longer be paying for the expenses on the car and that Matt would need to be responsible for any future expenses.

Several months later, I visited again with Robert. He recounted to me what happened after that, which I found quite interesting. "At first, Matt loudly complained while the car sat in the driveway for a couple of weeks," he related. "Since he didn't have money to buy gas, he eventually went out on his own and got a job! He was now able to pay for his own gas and insurance. The car no longer 'needed' all those repairs he wanted done." Robert not only realized the benefit of saving some money by not paying those expenses, but most importantly he was proud of the opportunity for accomplishment that this situation provided Matt.

At first, the exchange wasn't beneficial to either Robert or his son (although Matt may have disagreed). When Robert realized this, he adjusted the agreement for everyone's benefit.

So, just as life is always in a state of flux, so should be your exchanges.

The Importance of Being Consistent

Having just talked about flexibility, I also want to talk about consistency within your exchanges. I believe that consistency is one of the most important factors in raising children. Consistency within an exchange (your relationship) lets your child know where you are (or what they can get away with!). While providing flexibility in the context of setting each exchange, you as the parent *must* assume the responsibility to be consistent and to reset the terms of that exchange when necessary.

A mother who attended one of my seminars approached me during a break. "I tried something similar with my kids years ago," she said. "I even went on strike once to get them to stop taking advantage of me. It worked, but only for a week. When I quit putting the pressure on, everyone else quit as well." She wasn't consistent in her approach, so neither were the results.

A garden must be constantly cultivated or the weeds will quickly take over and ruin all the hard work you have done. It's the same with exchanges. Sometimes I forget and slip into old ways of doing things. I have to catch myself and correct my course. I know that my children will cheerfully take whatever they can get from me, whenever they can get it, without an exchange. So I must always be aware and consistent in our exchanges.

Hold Your Ground

"Stop right there, young man!" Stevie looks at his mom out of the corner of his eye and continues doing what he wants. Stevie's mom tries again. "Don't you move another step! No, No, N-N-O-O!" she continues. Moving a little slower now, but still watching his mom, Stevie keeps right on moving. "I mean it. Don't even think about it," she tries again. Without looking back, Stevie continues on his way. His mom, now weary of the whole situation and countless others like it, shrugs her shoulders. Then, in a tired voice, she says, "He never listens to me." And you know what? He knows that he doesn't have to. He hears the words and threats, but nothing ever happens—no consequences, no time out, no restrictions—just the same old words without actions.

Never *set an exchange that you are not willing* **and** *able to follow through with.* If these interactions between Stevie and his mother continue until he is sixteen, and little Stevie becomes Steve, what has his mom trained him to do when interacting with her? If you said ignore her, you're probably right. I believe that the consistency I have had with my children has been one of the main reasons that I have had success with my seven children, even as a single parent.

Putting it All Together

A Somewhat Typical Scenario

A friend of mine grew tired of her husband's empty threats with their two boys when they acted up in the car. When the kids were going at each other in the back seat, the dad would typically say, "If you don't stop that, we'll let you walk!" Or if the noise level got too high: "One more scream from you guys and we'll make you get out of the car." Did the kids ever listen? Of course not. They may have been in the middle of the Mojave Desert when the threats were made, but the kids knew that their dad would never actually make them walk.

Finally, my friend had had enough of her husband's inconsistencies. One day, after they picked the boys up at a ball game two miles from home, the fighting began as usual. Again, the dad made his threats. But this time, my friend followed through and insisted that her husband stop the car. The two teenage boys actually did have to walk home. They (and their dad) were fuming. But from then on, the parents never had to make threats about walking home. By bringing the father's inconsistency out on the table, things changed for the better.

Applying consistency within your exchanges is absolutely necessary. I know that with my children, they felt more at ease at home and in their relationships with me because there really weren't any hidden surprises. What they saw (so to speak), they knew they were getting. They could be assured that I would be up front and consistent with my expectations. This provided a foundation for an environment of peace and safety in our home and in our relationships.

Parenting on Purpose

Parenting should be *purposeful*. Make deliberate, conscious decisions about what you want to achieve. What result do you expect from the interactions you have with your child? When I originally searched for solutions with my children, I had two goals: one, that my children's lives should be the least negatively affected by any of my past choices and, two, to take some of the burden off of my shoulders (and mind). By specifically and purposefully considering what I wanted, solutions came.

Be mindful of what you truly want within the exchanges with your child. I would suggest that you periodically take some time to assess your exchanges. Here are some questions to consider:

- What do I want for my child?
- How is my relationship with my child?
- What are my motives behind the exchanges with my child?
- Will continuing the existing exchanges support the desired result?
- Are the exchanges "equitable" (relative to the ability and age of the child)?
- Are you aware of any hidden agendas within the exchange?

Putting it All Together

I have seen many parents overwhelm themselves chauffeuring their children to constant activities, such as soccer practice, piano lessons, dance lessons, and more. I see nothing wrong with having your children participate in these activities. What I do see as mistaken is the parent doing this out of obligation, guilt, or because it's what everyone else is doing. Some parents believe that they need to expose their children to these activities in order to be a good parent—that if they don't, somehow their children will be culturally or socially deprived. If a child isn't in the right school or doesn't have the right connections, they fear, he won't have options when he gets older.

But if there is too much going on and it does become overwhelming, all of this can be unhealthy for both the parent and the child. Again, appraising your exchanges and looking at the real motives and intents will help to ensure more peaceful and prosperous relationships.

> **Be mindful of what you truly want within the exchanges with your child**

Shortly after my divorce, when I went on welfare, I constantly fought my guilt, knowing that I didn't have the time or resources to provide these experiences for my children. As the years went by, I learned that living in the moment and creating the most beneficial exchanges with the resources that you have can be the best thing for you and your child. As I began to let go of the guilt and did the best I could, everything

The Parenting Exchange

worked out. Our children sometimes learn most effectively from the unintentional situations in life.

I was able to witness this while observing the success attained by my son Paul. He never went to preschool and always attended public schools. I never put him in an organized sport league outside of his public school (I had too many other younger children at home to take care of). On his middle school report cards, he had failing grades. For a time, he was being raised by a single welfare mother with six younger siblings. By the time he was a junior in high school, we had moved 10 times.

One might have thought Paul's opportunities severely limited. However, as I implemented the exchange system early in Paul's high school career, he found a way to succeed. By the end of high school, he was courted by several top colleges in the country. He ended up attending Princeton University and playing football for them. He has traveled the world and was a page for the State legislature. My other children have also been successful, even though I didn't have the opportunity to involve them in activities that I wished I could have.

So, as you consider how you will make your exchanges with your child, be present in the moment, in the reality of the present exchange. Consider what you feel will be of the most value for your child. In my case, I decided that my children needed a relatively sane mother more than they needed Girl Scouts. That was my motivating belief.

Putting it All Together

Unique Exchanges

As I talk to parents about these ideas, I have realized that what each parent wants from an exchange with his or her child is as unique as the child. Some parents just want to make it through the day without a phone call from the child's school. Others want their children to win beauty pageants. Some parents want good grades for children. Others just want to be good friends with their kids. Everyone is different, and everyone's desires are different. What sets this exchanged-based process apart is that it gives parents a tool that can be used in all of these scenarios.

Once you understand this, take the time to decide what you want. Clearly defining the most basic desires within your family can give you the foundation on which to set your exchanges and give you the results that you are seeking. If having a clean house is paramount to you, then set your exchanges with your child to help you get that. Find out what your child wants, and use that in your exchange to get your house clean.

The Assurance of Clarity

A lack of clarity can cause confusion for both parent and child and totally disrupt what could otherwise be an effective exchange. If the individuals involved have different expectations, each may think that the other person is not holding up his end when the problem is actually a

The Parenting Exchange

misunderstanding of the exchange. Clarity, particularly from the parent, will support an environment for trust to thrive.

> **Before putting exchanges into action, it's best to clarify the exchange with everyone involved.**

Let's start this discussion with a couple of fun little stories. A few years back, I had a sock problem with my girls. They were constantly wearing my socks, and I wasn't. I would go to my sock drawer, and it would be empty. I had to go my girls' room, find "their" socks and sort out which ones were mine. I did this over and over again until one day I thought of what I believed to be a great solution

Finally, when I had some time, I gathered all my socks together. Using a permanent laundry marker, I wrote the word "MOM" on all of my socks. I believed this would solve my sock problem. Everyone would now know whose socks were whose. But a few days later, as we sorted the family laundry, my sock solution came under question. My daughter Aleena was helping me sort the clothes and found my labeled socks. With a puzzled look on her face she asked, "Mom, why is the word 'wow' on some of these socks?" My girls still bring up this story and chuckle about it to this day.

You may not know how your child perceives what is clear to you. Before putting exchanges into action, it's best to clarify the exchange with everyone involved.

Paul, when he was seventeen, had been letting his household responsibilities slip, so I reminded him of the terms

Putting it All Together

of our exchange. I could tell that Paul wasn't very happy about it. Later in the day I overheard him complaining to a visiting friend of mine. "I can't believe that my mom is being so demanding. I have so much going on at school with homework and football practice," he moaned. "There's no way I can help around the house as much as Mom wants me to. I just don't have enough time."

When my friend saw that Paul felt genuinely overwhelmed, he suggested to him, "Can you spare one-half hour a day? That's really all she's asking for." Paul's facial expression immediately changed as he considered this, realizing that what he was saying was true. Paul then agreed, affirming, "Oh, I can do *that*."

"I think Paul assumed you wanted him to participate in some sort of slave labor camp," my friend later told me. Paul just needed to have my expectations clarified in more concrete terms (re-setting the exchange). He needed to know what the limit was on the contribution expected of him. Paul also needed his mother to make sure that she was being clearly understood.

Let's go back to the YouTube video of the father who shot his daughter's laptop. During his monologue, the dad clarified the family's expectations for his daughter. He broke it down to the specific amount of time he believed it should take his daughter to perform her tasks. The daughter might now see that the exchange she had with her father really wasn't that bad. In fact, it was beneficial to her.

I remember another time when I made an exchange with my son Paul when he wanted to borrow my car. We had an apricot tree that needed picking. I agreed that in exchange for a full bucket of picked, ripe apricots, he could use the car. Sure enough he completed his end of the task, so of course I needed to uphold mine. The only "duh" factor on my end was that the bucket was filled with all colors (green, yellow and orange) of fruit—I had forgotten that Paul was colorblind! As parents, we need to keep in mind that what we ask of our children should to be something that they are capable of.

Re-setting Exchanges

After I began using this exchange process with my children, I began to see some encouraging results. However, what sometimes would start out in promising ways would sometimes also revert back to old patterns. During this time, I was juggling many plates. I also had too many kids to try to monitor all of their behaviors, nor did I have a desire to do so. I recognized that the initial agreement of an exchange sometimes needed to be "re-set."

When Paul was sixteen, he had a girlfriend in a nearby town whom he wanted to spend time with. He asked to use my car to drive to her house so they could do their homework together. I consented, provided that he buy gasoline for the car and return home by 10:30 at night (setting the exchange). At first he kept the agreement, but soon he became careless about the curfew, often arriving home several hours late.

Paul regarded himself as a very honest person, yet he wasn't being honest with me by not keeping up his end of

Putting it All Together

agreement. So one day I told Paul that I had a problem with him. He asked what that was and I replied, "I want to know why you are lying to me."

"I don't lie to you," he replied (and in his mind he didn't). "When did I do that?"

I responded, "You lied about our exchange. You told me you would bring the car home by 10:30. That was our agreement. Since you haven't done that lately, you've broken our agreement, and it looks to me like you are lying."

Paul immediately understood what I meant. After that, he either arrived home on time or called home to renegotiate his arrival time. By helping Paul to recognize that he wasn't keeping up his end of the agreement, we were able to quickly solve the problem without getting into an argument.

"Getting Around the Arguments"

When my first book, *A Little Secret for Dealing with Teens*, was published, I came across several reviews of my book. For the most part, they were all favorable—until I stumbled upon a review on the Internet. At first I wasn't quite sure where the review came from or who wrote it. After some searching I learned that the review was written *by a teen*. It was entitled, "This 'Little Secret' shouldn't be out."

When I saw the title, my stomach went into a knot (why wouldn't they like *my* book?). Let me share with you the review:

The Parenting Exchange

> *I've glanced through a couple of parenting books (while bored out of my mind in a doctor's waiting room) and most of them seem to have a pretty good handle on reality.*
>
> *Jennie Hernandez' "A Little Secret for Dealing with Teens" is quite the opposite.*
>
> *She begins by giving parents a few scenarios she thinks they can relate to, such as a police officer at your door at 2 a.m. or getting into your car and noticing the front end has been mysteriously rearranged. Maybe it's me, but those don't seem like situation most teen-agers would be in. Those are the extreme, and would be handled much differently than average mistakes.*
>
> *This book is unrealistic when it comes to relationships between parents and their teens. I don't know teen-agers who sit down with their parents and make lists of what they expect of each other in terms of clothes and food. The author recommends this because it will supposedly show teens that they should give the parent something in return.*
>
> *This book basically told me this mother was trying too hard to get her kids to respect the rules and she found that she could get around the arguments by making exchanges—meaning she would give them something if they gave her something.*
>
> *Ms. Hernandez doesn't seem to know much about how teens think and act. She seems to say we are selfish and unwilling to listen to anything any adult says and, for the most part, that isn't true. Her way of dealing with teens may have worked for her, but I think it is unrealistic and worthless for other families. Most of the people I know are in a completely different mindset.*
>
> *I would not recommend this book to the parent of any teen.*

My favorite line of the review is: "she found that she could get around the arguments by making exchanges." She basically made my point. What parent of a teen, or any child, wouldn't want to build responsibility in their child while at the same time

Putting it All Together

minimizing the arguments? I've learned that this process really does do that. After a few months of integrating these exchange principles, arguments between my children and me were almost non-existent. From the perspective of a parent, I appreciate this as a wonderful gift.

Recently, I was having lunch with Marcos, a good friend of mine who had married, and now had a teenage stepson. Our lunch conversation turned to the recent changes in his relationship with his stepson, Alex. "At first," Marcos admitted, "the relationship was constantly strained. But I now understand that I was continually trying to control him and impose *my* agenda on him. I felt that I knew what was best for him. Looking back now, I still believe that I had and still have a better perspective and probably do know what's best for him, but I have also come to recognize that it is not my job to impose that on him or fix him, only to provide the environment for him to do his best."

"I would get hung up on things like his hair," he explained. "I didn't like his out-of-control style, so I would tell him to cut it or change it. Then we would end up in an argument. Now I accept that it is his choice to have any hairstyle that he chooses and that it really has nothing to do with me. I began to understand Alex's environment (work, teachers, etc.) will eventually provide him the feedback which will help him make the best decision on his hair style."

Marco and I then discussed how much easier and more productive it is to "focus on the exchange, not the other person," and how this process alleviates most tension within the exchange. "I realized that there was little need to concern myself with his choices until they negatively affected me or the family. We hardly ever have arguments anymore. What a relief!"

Benefits and Beyond (Home)

As your children internalize and implement this process, they will naturally apply it to their other relationships--outside of your home and family. This can be very helpful to them, especially as they prepare to go out into the world and learn to survive (and thrive). It helps them avoid being taken advantage of, because they will be aware of the reciprocity and equity that should be a part of all their relationships.

> **As your children internalize and implement this process, they will naturally apply it to their other relationships--outside of your home and family.**

During the years that my children were at home, I chuckled when I discovered that my kids (especially when they were teens) didn't put up with inequity in their relationships with their friends. One day I overheard Juliana visiting with her best friend Kelly. From what I could tell, Kelly had asked Juliana one too many times to give her answers for their homework. Juliana finally pointed out to Kelly that she never did that for *her*, so from then on, she would have to get her own answers. Kelly was upset and didn't talk to

Putting it All Together

Juliana for a few days. Finally Kelly called and apologized. She realized that she had been taking advantage of the friendship and said she wouldn't do it anymore. They are still best friends to this day.

In high school, my daughter Christina was majorly involved in cheerleading and was captain most of the time. Needless to say, there was plenty of drama between the cheerleaders. When the cheer coaches invited Christina to be captain, they said things to her like: "We think you will be a great captain because you don't let the other girls take advantage of you." Or, "We want you in this role because you don't seem to get involved in the petty games that most of the other girls do."

I implemented this process with my family when Christina was about three years old. I have watched her apply it not only with cheer but in most of the relationships in her life. She has lost some friends due to bringing up the inequity of the exchanges. Some of these friends came back later and acknowledged that what she brought up was true. They then reengaged their friendships and have become some of her best friends for life. Others never tried to work it out but, according to Christina, it was for the best since they didn't want to deal with the reality of what was going on anyway.

A Simple Awareness

Awareness changes things. I know that my children are more conscious in all aspects of their lives because of the

The Parenting Exchange

awareness that their exchanges have instilled in them. They have discovered that exchanges are constantly a part of all of their relationships. This realization came about as our family consistently brought the underlying expectations of our exchanges out in the open. My kids just can't ignore the obvious: they must do something for what they get; they must take part in the exchange, if only to say "thank you."

A few years back, a former coworker of mine invited Christina to go with their family for an outing as they had a daughter the same age. Later, my friend and her husband shared with me how courteous and appreciative Christina had been during their time together. They expressed that they had never met a child who had shown so much gratitude. They were taken aback by her concern that they might be spending too much money on her.

Of course this made me feel good. I am proud of my children. I could say it's just great genetics, or it's because they are wonderful people. But I know that by making my children aware of hidden costs and exchanges, they are more grateful for what they get and want to give more to others in return.

When teaching my seminars, I often have parents ask me how I can expect these things of my children when all their friends follow different ideologies. Some people have even asked if my children are embarrassed around their friends because our family's expectations are so different. My answer, I believe, surprises them. Many of my children's friends would spend more time at our home than at their own. We have a lot of fun, and we all get along pretty well. When this exchange-based process works, it begins to feel very natural. My children don't do without; they simply share the responsibility of helping them get what they want.

Parenting As a Role

Throughout your life, you participate in many roles, such as being a son or daughter, a spouse, a cousin, a teacher, a student or any number of other roles. When you give birth or a child becomes part of your family, you will take on the role of being a parent. A role is a set of expected behaviors as well as rights and obligations. What the role of a parent entails will have different meanings for different families.

I have known people who have completely defined themselves by their roles as parents. Much of their personal identities is wrapped around this role. However, if a parent becomes too personally invested, it can become difficult to separate personal feelings and desires from the role of parenting.

A parent should be able to separate his or her identity from the job of being a parent. I still remember the day that I had the "aha" moment—when I came to this realization. I recognized that this was a healthy perspective with several benefits. By viewing my role as a parent from this perspective, I was able to let go of my ego and

> **A parent should be able to separate his or her identity from the job of being a parent.**

The Parenting Exchange

personal investment in the outcome of my parenting. It was liberating in the sense that I could parent with a sense of detachment. The exchanges with my children became more about how it would be rewarding for them instead of what I personally wanted.

Over time, it became evident that this approach was more empowering for my children. I focused on helping them become independent of me. This provided them with a greater opportunity to set their own direction in their lives. As they grew older, their goals and ambitions were theirs, not mine. When the time came, it also made things a little less painful when my children left home, since I wasn't completely defined by my role as a parent. Now that they are all out of the house, I have worked myself out of the job of parent and my children are now my best friends.

I knew a couple who wanted to be "forever" parents, since this was how they came to define themselves. They had four grown children, all still living with them. The parents provided them with a nice house to live in, all expenses paid. These adult children got their clothes washed, meals cooked, and house cleaned while driving nicer cars than their parents.

But this scenario came at a cost. By being a "permanent" parent, you have "permanent" children. These adult children were trapped in dependency, persuaded by parents who had an unhealthy need to keep their children dependent. At times, what appears to be generosity can be selfishness on the part of the parents. Be sure to be aware of the reasons and intentions behind your exchanges with your children.

Putting it All Together

Being the Butler

Another way that parents get caught in inequitable exchanges with their children is by interacting with them in set roles. If you were to hire a butler to answer your door and drive you around, you would always expect him to perform those services no matter what—that's his job. Children often do the same thing with their parents. They expect the parents to perform predetermined services no matter what. Often, this does not make an equitable exchange possible. Yet if everyone will let go of these predetermined roles and focus on making exchanges work within *each* situation, they'll be pleasantly surprised at the results, and wonderful relationships develop.

The following is a true story related by "Tom," a friend of mine. He tells of an experience he had with his thirteen-year-old daughter. His chance to "work himself out of a parenting job" came earlier to him than he expected.

Years ago, Tom's daughter Amy approached him saying, "Dad, I need to talk with you—just you and me." So they talked. "Dad," Amy asked, "isn't it true that I pretty much do everything what you would consider the right way?"

"Well, yes, that's pretty much true," he admitted. She had good grades, did her work around the house, stayed out of trouble, helped her parents with the younger children, and did a very good job of being responsible.

"So let's quit doing this parent-child thing," she petitioned. After considering her unique and genuine request, he agreed. He didn't quit being a parent or stop loving her, but he did allow her to be independent in the majority of her decisions for her life—and it worked. Today, she has done well in life and now is a parent herself. She has since expressed to her father how much she appreciated his respect for her wishes to take charge of her life at an early age.

Some parents may not agree that this is good parenting. However, this unique exchange achieved early what many parents want to eventually accomplish with their children—independence.

> **Your eventual goal should be to stop parenting.**

For a few years, I was a parent to a teenage stepson who was deaf. Because of his specialness, I took a more active role in parenting for those years more than I normally would have. Each child is different and you follow what each individual child needs most. Your eventual goal should be to stop "parenting," even though you never stop being their parent.

A Different World (Than You Grew Up In)

Every generation of parents thinks the world they grew up in was very different from the world their kids are growing up in. I would tend to agree, but I would also say that the world kids are now growing up in is exponentially different, due to major

Putting it All Together

advances in technology. These innovations touch almost all of us throughout each day.

With this ever-changing world of technology, I find that many parents are unsure of how to find a balance of being a responsible parent while allowing their kids to connect to this virtual, changing world. There seem to be unlimited options that continue to multiply. So, as children become more immersed in these realms, how can a parent effectively marry the two—being a responsible parent while accepting and incorporating the virtual electronic world that our kids are such a part of?

A major issue that parents have is a fear (or a reality) that their children are becoming disconnected from everyday, face-to-face relationships and caught in their own virtual worlds. This could be a child buried in a video game for hours on end, a teen constantly on her cell phone texting, or a kid forever on Facebook.

Communication has shifted from verbal to electronic.

I remember years ago when my young "tween" daughter, Emily, basically believed everything she saw or read on the Internet. I tried explaining to her that things aren't always as they seem. One day she began chatting online with a "boy" who seemed too good to be true. He supposedly

The Parenting Exchange

lived nearby. He had recently moved to our little town from the same state we used to live in. He was just the right age, and so on. She asked me to come look at their conversation, because she wanted to know if she could give him her phone number at his request. I was a little suspicious. I told her that she really had no idea who she was talking to. "Yes, I do. He told me right here," she said, pointing to the screen. She wouldn't believe that this person wasn't who he said he was. Two days later, her female cousin confessed that she had been pretending to be this boy.

Emily was in a fantasy world; to her it was real. If our kids are allowed to stay in these worlds without having to come out and deal with reality, then their thinking becomes warped so that they think their fantasy worlds are reality.

Parents need specific, practical tools to use to connect with their children.

I wrote my first book shortly after the Columbine High School shooting in Colorado. At the time, there was a lot of discussion on why this happened. I remember hearing a news interview with an "expert" about the shooting. He reported that there had been a much larger public response to this shooting than to any other news topic he had ever covered. One of his main points was that this shooting had taken place in an area that many would say is the "American Dream," a safe place. The question was then asked, "How could this happen to these kinds of people in this type of neighborhood?"

Putting it All Together

As these questions were being asked, there was also a lot of blame going around. People were blaming the movie industry, the media, the Internet, schools, and lax gun-control laws. Ultimately, much of the blame went to the parents. I don't know if I agree with this assessment, but I do believe that parents need specific, practical tools to use to connect with their children.

You may struggle to communicate with their different interests that keep them in their own worlds.

As you know, I am not a psychologist or a sociologist; I am a mother. I believe that parents owe it to their children to teach them how to assume responsibility for their own actions. I don't believe that we can blame society, the media, or insufficient laws for the behavior of our children. I will recommend that you use this valuable tool of equitable exchanges to help your child come out of his *virtual* world and deal with *real-life* exchanges.

Contracts for the Real World

Let me share with you a good example of how a mother did just this. A recent article tells of a mother giving her thirteen-year-old son his first iPhone. As the article reports, "It came with strings attached." This mom required that her son, upon acceptance of the phone, sign an 18-point contract outlining the terms of "exchange." Included in the first point: "It is my

The Parenting Exchange

phone. I bought it. I pay for it. I am loaning it to you." Here she is bringing up her terms for this exchange.

The contract continues "You must share passwords with a parent, answer their calls, hand over said device early on school nights and a little later on weekends. You must avoid hurtful texts and porn and pay for a replacement if your phone falls into the toilet, smashes on the ground, or vanishes into thin air." Of the latter she advises her teen, "Mow a lawn, stash some birthday money. It will happen, you should be prepared."

If the son accepts the terms of this exchange, he will probably have more awareness, take on more responsibility, and know that his mom has the "right" to take back the phone if he doesn't adhere to the conditions of the agreement. For me, this is a wonderful example of the old adage: an ounce of prevention is worth a pound of cure. I am convinced from my experience raising my children that this contract will save this mom far more than a *pound of cure.* (And of course, the son doesn't have to accept these terms—or the phone--if he doesn't want to.)

With the advent of the Internet we are all now part of a very large, interconnected community. Throughout this book, I have shared stories of how some parenting decisions, with the help of the Internet, have gone viral. At times, when a parent makes a parenting decision that is outside the norm, it catches the attention of not only thousands but even millions. I guess this could be a good or a bad thing. Many parents may now feel concerned that if they make an uncommon parenting decision it could end up on YouTube.

I know that for my family and me, I need to make choices because I believe they are the best for us, not because of what others are doing. I laugh a little thinking of when I was a child (and I'm sure you may have had a similar experience) and my dad would say, "If all of your friends jumped off a cliff, would you do it too?" or something similar. I believe this same principle applies to parenting—just because society tells you to do something or everyone is doing something, does that mean it is right for you? I also suppose that many of our parenting choices are made from these kinds of preconceived expectations.

Applied Science (Fairs)

One of my local papers publishes a weekly column written by a parenting blogger. A few months ago, the topic was about school science fairs. The article began: "Any other parents out there in science fair hell?" Well, when I read this first sentence, I pretty much surmised how this article was going to play out. Sure enough, it mostly talked about the undue burden that the science fair would bestow onto the parents. This mom/blogger explains that her seventh and fourth graders' "efforts have forced them to express themselves very precisely, and perform small steps over time to meet the deadline for this rather large project."

Her next point is where she and I part ways. "But of course, none of this educational magic happens if children are just left to their own devices. Nor do gentle verbal reminders

The Parenting Exchange

accomplish much," she continues. "What we've learned—and I'm guessing we are not alone here—is that the only way science fair projects get completed on time and even remotely resembling what the instructions say they must, is if one or both parents crack the whip over the little scientists' heads on a daily (hourly?) basis for two straight months."

I don't know about you, but when I read this, my first thought was: I wasn't the one who signed on for the science fair--my kids did.

She and her husband repeatedly reminded the kids during their Christmas break to complete their projects. Her son (who she describes as a science whiz), instead of doing this, "snuck onto the computer to browse YouTube for Lego Star Wars videos, play Lego Star Wars games or create wildly colorful Power Point films about Lego Star Wars at every opportunity all through his break. Somehow, it took parental temper tantrums to get him to log off Lego and tune into science fair. Because he was in a hurry to return to All Things Lego Star Wars, he tried to write up a simple-as-possible hypothesis."

When the teacher sent an email requesting more specifics from the son, he "got mad at *me* for telling him to make her suggested changes. Hey, don't shoot the messenger!" she told him (which leads me to assume that she is the one reading and responding to the email sent to her son).

At this point of the article, I'm thinking, "And she's a professional parenting writer?" In my mind, I begin to "plug in" the five steps of my parenting exchange process into this scenario. But before I go there, let me share the rest of the article. The next part of her discussion was about her daughter and how she, as the mom, had to purchase balloons and help her daughter fill them with water for the experiment. Apparently, it was "about 30 seconds before all the balloons broke and the kids were bickering."

She continues: "I gently suggested tackling a different topic, and even pulled three very simple ideas off the Internet, and that triggered a major hissy fit. The meltdown was exacerbated by Daughter's strong desire to meet a friend outside—or watch Disney Channel, or invite a friend over to mess around with the karaoke machine. It took several hours for her to calm down enough to even have a conversation, let alone plot out a new project."

The blog ends with her asking, "But really, there ought to be a law. If you gave birth, doesn't that exempt you from science fair duty? What helps keep the kids on task?"

In answer to her questions, I have a few points. First, I do believe that having given birth exempted me from science fair *duty*. This "duty" belongs to the child whose project it is. In response to what helps keep the kids on task, the kids do. My answers may seem idealistic, but they worked for me. I just used the five-step exchange model.

Applying the Exchange Process

In the following paragraphs, I will insert points from this parenting blog to illustrate the five-step *parenting exchange*

The Parenting Exchange

process. In her blog, the author poses some questions. Using the exchange model, I will provide some answers.

1. All Relationships are Exchanges

It is a given that she and her children are in an exchange.

2. Exchanges are Run by Expectations

From what I can glean from the article here are some possible kids' expectations:

I don't really need to take responsibility for my science fair project because my parent(s) will do that for me.

If I become distracted long enough, my mom will solve my problems and possibly even do my work for me.

Not only do I not have to do the work, I can bicker with my sibling, complain about the work, and get mad at my mom when she makes suggestions of what I should be doing.

You may be able to find more of these, but you get the point.

Possible mom's expectations:

If I leave my kids to their own devices, they won't know how to do their projects.

The only way for the project to be completed on time is by me constantly "cracking the whip" (for 2 months straight).

Putting it All Together

My children have expectations to keep using all of the electronic equipment we as parents have purchased and using large amounts of my thoughts and energy while also having the right to throw "major" hissy fits.

Again, you could probably find even more, but the point is made.

3. Some Expectations Running Exchanges are Hidden

In these examples, you will see some hidden expectations imbedded in the actions of this family. As I explained earlier, sometimes these are even hidden from ourselves. I believe this mother really does make the assumption that without parents' help, this is an impossible task for her children; so, this exchange is played out according to that assumption. Her kids somehow know this to be the case, so they take advantage of it. If you were to go back and read this article with this in mind, the pieces fall into place.

A hidden expectation of the children may be: *Mom is the one who wants the science project completed, not me, so I will let her take most of the responsibility and do most of the work, and I don't have to feel guilty.* This may explain why the kids played games with their friends and even threw fits to get out of taking responsibility for completing the project.

4. Bringing the Hidden Expectations "Out-on-the-Table" Always Changes the Exchange.

Let's imagine a scenario. What if mom had said something like: "This is the fourth year of science fairs in our family. If history repeats itself, I'll be doing the majority of the work. So, before this happens, let's sit down and talk about who will be responsible for what. If you don't follow through with your part, the consequences will not be as they have been in the prior years." She could then remind her kids that what she calls "the" computer is really the parents' computer, since they purchased it. She might also point out that the project is the kids' project, not the parents' project.

I'm not saying that kids won't need outside help to complete their projects, but that it should be the kids' responsibility to figure out how to accomplish this. They may need to initiate some exchanges with their parents or even others that have expertise in this area to help them get it done. By having an open discussion about the motives and responsibilities connected to this project and frankly discussing how it will all play out, the exchanges would surely be different.

5. Focus of Getting the Exchange to Work, Not on Changing the Other Person.

This last step requires taking a step back to identify the exchange that you care about. In the context of this exchange, I would first ask the question, why are the kids participating in

Putting it All Together

the science fair in the first place? Is it because the kids want to or the parents or both? Once this is determined, then the exchange process begins. If either of the kids really doesn't want to do it, then, as a parent, decide if it is worth the efforts of the exchange to make this happen. If you believe it is, then let your kids know what the parameters are for you supporting them.

The author asks: How have science fairs gone in your household and what helps keep the kids on task? Well, for me, science fairs were barely a hiccup. My kids did their own work and if they needed any help, they either asked a friend or neighbor or, if they needed my help, they would do something for me in exchange—as to not put an extra burden on me. The great thing about this way of solving the "science fair duty" is that I don't get upset if my child wants to watch TV or play video games or whatever they want to do (not focusing on the other person and what they want, just getting the exchange to work). I just remind them of our exchanges, which usually involve them not using "my" TV or having free-time computer use until their work is done.

If one of my kids had thrown a "major hissy fit," such as the daughter did in this story, I would shut down access to things that the writer mentioned: watching the Disney Channel, inviting a friend to mess around with the karaoke machine, or inviting a friend over. As those involved in these exchanges get used to this arrangement, the arguments go away and the children learn that their homework is *theirs*. Again, this then translates into a mindset of responsibility—not only for their schoolwork, but for all aspects of their lives.

A Different Process

I did a search today on Amazon.com to see how many parenting books were listed. 136,036 came up in the search results for "parenting books." So why would I want to change this number to 136,037? What difference would or could my book have? How is this parenting process any different?

Last week I was visiting with "Dr. Richards," a pastor of a local church who works with formerly incarcerated individuals and their families. I was sharing with him a little about my parenting process and discussing a possible speaking opportunity. During our conversation he commented on some parenting classes that many of the families he works with are required to attend. These mandated classes instruct compliance with what is minimally, legally required of parents—their responsibility to provide shelter, food, and clothing.

As the conversation continued, I smiled and shared that in my parenting, I also believe that parents are obligated to provide the "basic necessities" for their children, which I expanded to include nurturing and love. Dr. Richards then commented, "You are going a couple of steps beyond what is required in this other parenting process. Not only do you teach what is required by law, but you also teach how to go beyond this—what children genuinely need."

Putting it All Together

As a five-step, model-based approach, the *parenting exchange* incorporates a multi-level, "holistic" strategy. This process achieves results that a method focusing on basic "rules" or preset expectations never could. At a workshop I recently attended, I met another author of a parenting book. After the workshop, we exchanged our books. He commented, "I'm sure our books and ideas are quite similar." When I later read his book, I saw that he had some great parenting ideas, but our processes were different. His book included chapters on very specific "to-dos," such as how to schedule appointments, getting organized, and his thoughts on excuses and absences from school. I think that if a parent were to follow these steps, it *would* be of help. How the *parenting exchange* process differs, though, is that a parent may choose a different approach in each of these circumstances—depending on the child, the result desired, or the context of each situation.

The Bug Guy

Last summer, our pest control technician, Jeff, was making the monthly service call to our home. When he was finished, he came to the door for me to sign the receipt. As we talked, he told me about his three children in middle and high school, and I told him a bit about my parenting book and the exchange process. "Oh, I already do that with my kids," he responded. "If they do their assigned chores, they get an allowance at the end of the week."

The Parenting Exchange

"I'm glad that you have this exchange in place with your kids, but let me share how my process is a little different," I said. "You assign the chores for your kids and determine the amount to pay, correct?"

"Yes, that's how we do it."

"At our house," I explained, "it's up to my kids to figure out, and come to me, to solve how to get what they want. There's no pre-set exchange. Let me give you an analogy. When you were looking for a job, did the company you work for come to your house and knock on your door to ask you if you wanted to work for them?"

"Well no." he answered with surprise. "I had to apply for this position and interview before they hired me."

"Well, this is how this *parenting exchange* process works. The responsibility is on the child to initiate what he or she wants and to either take responsibility to get it or offer an exchange to someone else if he or she needs outside help. Just like you, no one handed you the job--you had to take the initiative to get it."

This small distinction makes an amazing difference. When I began working with my children in this new way, all of our lives shifted. This small shift in *your* parenting can help your child become happier and more responsible while lightening your duties as a parent. Win-win!

Not Always the Easiest

Putting it All Together

To be successful in applying this process and achieving positive results with your children, you, as a parent, will sometimes need to make difficult choices. As I apply this process with my children, I have to let go of my ego, let go of what others may think, and let go of many social norms. When I do this, I experience a profound shift in my relationships with my children. They experience remarkable results. They have discovered that they need to take responsibility for what they need and want out of life. If they don't, nobody is going to hand it to them--no fairy godmother! They understand that there is no entitlement.

> **To be successful, you, as a parent, will sometimes need to make difficult choices.**

When I submitted the draft of my first parenting book to the publisher, they recommended that I omit the following story about my daughter Linda. It's about a decision that we made together to solve a difficult situation. The publishers thought that how we handled it was a little extreme. Perhaps it was, but it was a choice that worked for us for this particular situation.

I decided to leave it in the book, as it illustrates the essence of the overall exchange process. It demonstrates how a child internalized the principles of exchange and responsibility and illustrates a parent letting go of pre-conceived solutions.

Several years ago, when my daughter Linda was fourteen, I discovered that she and her young friends had been having drinking parties. I then learned that most of the drinking occurred at the home of one of the friends, Sara, because her single parent was seldom home. I felt a need to intervene, believing that my daughter was much too young to be drinking alcohol.

I didn't confront Linda about it right away. Later that evening, after I called her home from Sara's house, Linda and three of her friends arrived at our house and immediately disappeared into Linda's room. I overheard their conversation as I walked down the hall. The friends were pressuring Linda to do something she didn't want to do, and they advised her to lie to me about it. At this point I interrupted them and sent the three girls home after telling them I had overheard them talking. I sent Linda to the kitchen to do the dishes, which gave her time to think.

Shortly after this I found Linda crying at the kitchen sink. "I need to go away," she said. "I need to get away from these people. They keep making me do things I don't want to do." I understood what she meant. We lived in a very small town, and there was almost no way to avoid being around these friends.

So, she and I went out to get a bite to eat to discuss the matter. "Can you get by until the end of the school year and be ok with this situation?" I asked. "We will be moving to California then."

"No," she said. "I need to leave now. If I don't, I won't be able to deal with all of this." At the young age of fourteen, Linda had successfully identified a solution to a very difficult problem. Within a week, we agreed and arranged for her to move to California earlier than the rest of the family to live with an aunt until we arrived. There, she found plenty of new

Putting it All Together

friends. The move gave her a chance to blossom in wonderful ways we couldn't have imaged before. She accomplished things I didn't even know she could do.

A month after my talk with Linda, the parents of the other girls recognized that they needed to deal with the problem, as it continued to get worse. They then planned a meeting for all of the parents to discuss how to deal with their children. At our house, the problem was solved, and my daughter was the one who created the solution.

> **Regardless of the problems you have with your children, this process can help.**

I recognize that this solution isn't one that a lot of parents could or would choose. I know that many parents have problems with their children that involve serious situations such as drinking, drugs, or sex that often require professional advice and help. But, regardless of the problems you have with your child, this process can help. The key is to maintain the consistency of exchanges with your child. Linda made a major, responsible decision because I had maintained a consistency for many years with her. She learned certain rules in her life. Perhaps your child will begin to choose to live his or her life differently if he or she knows you will always be consistent and not facilitate unwise choices.

What if a teenage girl *knows* that if she became pregnant, her mother wouldn't raise that child or have them live in her home (or in other words, have mom take responsibility for the teenager's actions)? Perhaps then the daughter would know that her "real" options may be for her to go to work and take care of the child on her own, get married, or give the baby up for adoption. A child *knowing* this can definitely be preventive medicine. Teens who choose to drink, if it is by their own choice or that of their peers, will always need to be responsible for those choices in their exchanges with you as their parent. Are you helping them by letting them use a car to go out? How about giving them an allowance that gives them money to buy these things?

You can't always control your children, especially as they become adults, but you can control the consistency of your exchanges. Your child can and will make bad decisions, but you as a parent need to hold true to your rules, expectations, and exchanges. This consistency and flexibility in problem solving is key to making this process work.

Conclusion: It's Up to You

As I said at the beginning of the book, I created this process to prevent my kids from failing and me from going crazy (I'm paraphrasing). But so much more came from this. Not only did my children not fail, they achieved success. Some were successful in school, some in sports, and some in other capacities such as music, art, and cooking. Yet *my* favorite reward came as I experienced the love and respect that my children grew to have for each other and for me. Throughout the years, they have truly treated each other with kindness and respect. I'm not saying that there weren't disagreements from time to time, but I was amazed at how they grew to treat each other—and me—as best friends.

When you apply these exchange concepts, you will notice results immediately. Over time and with consistent use of the exchange-based approach, you will see a change in your child's attitude and life. What parent wouldn't want to see his child performing housework without even being asked, instead of arguing and then still not getting it done?

The exchange process explained in this book can be used in many ways. You can use it to solve just one problem you are having with your child, or you can completely transform your relationship with him or her. You can even carry this process into your other relationships. I had a friend use these exchange principles to restructure the management principles of his company. How you use the exchange-based process is entirely up to you.

The Parenting Exchange

Because every parent-child relationship is different, the results of applying this process will be unique. What happened in my own family was incredible! The magical quality of the process has a life of its own. The contrast between how things started out and how they became after making these changes was one of the most significant transformations that I have ever experienced.

My desire is that you and your family will also have success and amazing results as you implement the *parenting exchange*.

www.ingramcontent.com/pod-product-compliance
Lightning Source LLC
Chambersburg PA
CBHW061948070426
42450CB00007BA/1092